WIRING
YOUR MODEL RAILROAD

Larry Puckett

KALMBACH BOOKS

Kalmbach Books
21027 Crossroads Circle
Waukesha, Wisconsin 53186
www.KalmbachHobbyStore.com

All photos by the author except where otherwise noted.

Published in 2015
19 18 17 16 15   1 2 3 4 5

Manufactured in China

ISBN: 978-1-62700-175-5
EISBN: 978-1-62700-176-2

Editor: Jeff Wilson
Book Design: Tom Ford
Technical Editor: Hal Miller
Illustrator: Rick Johnson

Library of Congress Control Number: 2014958387

Contents

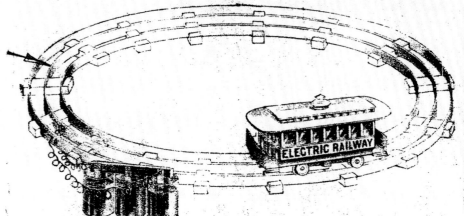

Classic Trains magazine collection

CHAPTER ONE

Basics of wiring

The first electrically powered model train actually was a trolley introduced in 1897 by Carlisle and Finch. This ad, from an 1897 issue of *The Electrical Engineer*, shows it powered by storage batteries; a hand-cranked dynamo (price: $7.50) was also available to power the trolley.

In 1897, Carlisle and Finch produced the first electric toy train, actually a trolley, **1**. These early trains ran off DC power provided by wet-cell batteries, which the owners had to build themselves! Ever since, model railroaders have spent an inordinate amount of time finding ways to power, wire, and control their locomotives and layouts.

Throughout the 1930s and most of the 1940s, the pages of *The Model Railroader* magazine were filled with articles discussing the merits of AC vs. DC power, batteries vs. transformers, two- vs. three-rail track and wiring, wound-field vs. permanent-magnet motors, signaling, and a host of other issues. By the late 1940s, manufacturers were finally producing power packs that could be plugged into a wall outlet to provide variable DC power to operate trains. During the 1950s a large array of locomotives and rolling stock kits became available, and HO trains running on track with two rails and DC power rapidly became the standard for most scale model railroaders.

With continued growth of the hobby during the 1960s and 1970s, innovation in methods of operation and control came to the front. Allen McClelland built his groundbreaking Virginian & Ohio model railroad and incorporated a new operating concept where model engineers actually walked along with their trains as they traversed the layout. This approach was aided when GE introduced the Astrac command control system in 1963, allowing modelers to simultaneously operate up to five locomotives on the same track. Although Astrac was discontinued in 1965, it set the stage for later command-control designs of the 1970s and 1980s by Digitrack 1600, Dynatrol, CTC-16, and various other command control systems.

By the mid-1990s, advancements in electronics made introduction of the Digital Command Control (DCC) protocol possible with standardization by the National Model Railroad Association (NMRA). With support for up to 10,000 locomotive addresses, modelers could operate as many locomotives as they could supply power to. During the past 20 years, DCC has become the default system for control of model trains, and manufacturers now commonly offer locomotives with factory-installed DCC decoders—many with sound.

In spite of all these advancements in technology and methods, for now (and the immediate future) we're still

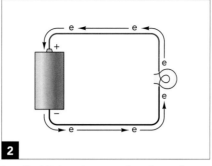

2

In a flashlight, electrons flow from the negative pole of the battery through the bulb and to the positive pole of the battery.

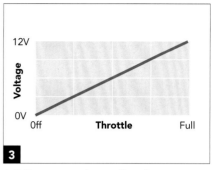

3

A DC power pack supplies electrons in a fairly stable pattern flowing in one direction.

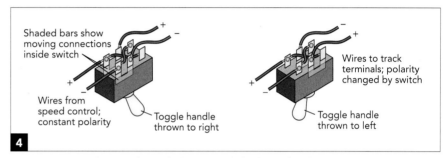

4

A reversing switch is easily made by wiring a double-pole, double-throw (DPDT) switch using this criss-cross pattern.

running wires to make it all happen, and that will be a major focus of this book. However, there is a lot more to operating a model railroad than just hooking up two wires to the track and pushing the go button. We will also look at the current state of the art in train control technology, accessories, operation, and design, and take on a few special projects. So let's begin with some of the basics that we can build upon later.

Electrical basics

Since everything that follows in this book in one way or another deals with how we use and control electricity, let's make sure we're all starting on the same level as far as understanding basic principles. The electricity we depend on to run our trains and associated equipment consists of electrons moving through wires. These electrons move from areas of high concentration at the negative pole of the circuit to areas of lower concentration at the positive pole. The best example of this is a simple battery-powered flashlight where electrons flow from the negative electrode though the light bulb to the

positive electrode, creating light and a little heat along the way, **2**. Replace the light bulb with a motor and you have the basic circuit for running a model locomotive.

Electricity is measured in terms of *volts* (V), which in effect is a measure of the pressure with which electrons are pushed through a circuit. We also have to consider the amount of electrons being moved and this is measured as *amperes* (amps, A) or *milliamps* (mA)—a milliamp is a thousandth (.001) of an amp. We'll learn more about how we measure these values in later chapters.

Electric power comes in two varieties, *direct current* (DC) and *alternating current* (AC). The earlier flashlight example shows DC power, which is easy to produce using batteries. Consequently, when they first started installing motors in model trains, that's what Carlisle and Finch used. However, keeping those batteries charged was a problem, so they later released a water-powered DC generator that could be attached to a household water line. In later years, DC generators powered by AC motors

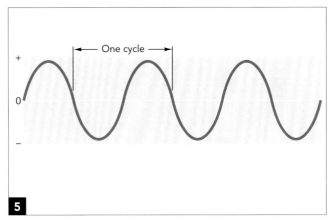

5

Household AC constantly reverses its direction of flow at a rate of 60 times per second, creating a sine wave.

6

This Model Rectifier Corp. Tech 7 is an example of a typical power pack that supplies DC for scale model trains.

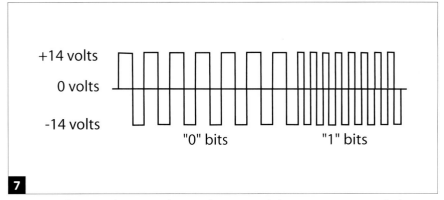

7

The power for Digital Command Control is a type of alternating current with the digital signal as part of it. It is much higher frequency than household AC.

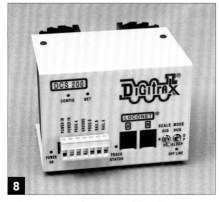

8

DCC command stations, like this Digitrax DCS 200, track the status of all locomotives and functions and create the digital signal to control them.

running off household AC power were even used to recharge batteries and operate trains. Batteries provided a good way to store the DC power, which could be varied using a simple rheostat, thus allowing modelers to control the speed of the locomotive. Many model railroaders continued to use batteries well into the 1940s—for example, Frank Ellison used surplus passenger-car batteries on his well-known Delta Lines O scale layout.

The good thing about DC is that the electrons only move in one direction, providing a stable flow of power to the track as the throttle is advanced, **3**, which makes it ideal for controlling small electric motors in trains. When electrons flow in one direction through the motor the locomotive travels in a set direction. If you reverse the direction in which electrons are flowing through the motor, the motor rotates in the opposite direction and the locomotive changes direction. This flow of

electrons can be easily reversed using a specially wired double-pole, double-throw (DPDT) switch, **4**.

Your house wiring is 120-volt AC power. The difference with AC is that the electrons regularly change their direction of flow, first moving forward and then backward. In the U.S., this frequency is 60 times per second, so it is referred to as 60-cycle AC, **5**.

In the early 1900s, as more and more homes were wired for AC electricity, some model train manufacturers began to design locomotives that could operate using it. Some early models actually ran on the full 110 volts! Fortunately, small step-down transformers began to appear, making it possible to drop the operating voltage and current down to safe levels. Many O and S gauge model trains (those still considered "toy trains") still use AC power.

One problem with using AC power for operating model trains is the reversing nature of its flow. You

can't simply throw a reversing switch to change the direction of locomotive movement. Instead you have to stop the locomotive, throw a sequencer switch either in the locomotive or controller, and then increase power to it. An interruption in power or a short circuit can cause the reversing sequencer to activate. This along with other shortcomings made DC increasingly popular among scale model railroaders, and that will be the focus of this book.

Power packs

Power packs, **6**, are the devices that convert household 120V AC power into low-voltage DC power and provide controls for running model locomotived. A power pack uses a transformer to reduce the AC household voltage and current to safe levels—usually 16V and 1A, but a bit higher for scales larger than HO. The

9

Boosters take the control signal from the command station and boost it to the final voltage supplied to the track.

10

Most DCC throttles are hand-held devices. They communicate with the command station to control locomotives and and other devices.

11

Mobile DCC decoders translate the control signal from the command station and convert AC track power to the DC power needed to operate the locomotive and functions.

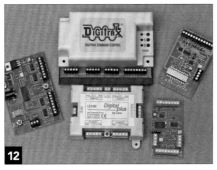

12

Stationary or accessory decoders decode the control signal from the command station and convert track power to DC to operate switches, lights, and other electrically operated accessories.

13

Track comes in a number of different sizes based on the height of the rails—for example, code 83 rail is .083" high. Here are pieces of HO track in (from left) code 70, 83, and 100.

AC output from the transformer passes through a rectifier, which converts it to DC. A circuit breaker is often included to cut off power in case of short circuits, and more advanced models may include a thermal (heat-sensitive) breaker to prevent damage in case of overheating.

Output voltage is varied to control locomotive speed using a rheostat or potentiometer, visible to the modeler as a lever or control knob on the case. Another important control is a direction switch, which allows you to control the direction the locomotive will travel. Most packs also have an on-off switch.

Screw terminals are provided to attach wire feeds. These include a pair of terminals for variable DC which are connected to the track and a pair of terminals for constant AC to power accessories such as lights and switch machines. Some power packs also

include a pair of terminals that provide constant DC.

Most companies that produce train sets (Athearn, Atlas, Bachmann, Kato, Model Power, and others) include a power pack with the set. These train-set power packs often are very basic and primarily suitable for running the locomotive included in the set. More advanced power packs with sophisticated electronics and higher power ratings are available from Model Rectifier Corp. and others. Some high-end packs offer momentum and braking for enhanced locomotive operation. Chapter 2 goes into more detail on basic DC control.

Digital Command Control

Digital Command Control (DCC) has grown rapidly since its introduction to the U.S. market in the mid-1990s. Command control systems allow several throttles to independently

control multiple locomotives on a single section of track without block divisions.

The big difference between DCC and earlier analog command control systems is that DCC's digital signal is embedded in the track power, **7**. Popular analog systems such as CTC16 had a small 3V analog command signal added on top of the 10V track power. This small signal was susceptible to electronic noise and crosstalk and it could only control locomotive speed and direction. With DCC, the digital signal is part of the track power, so is less susceptible to noise issues. More importantly, because it is digital, more information can be imbedded in it, allowing control of numerous functions.

A DCC system comprises several components: a power supply, a command station, boosters, throttles, decoders, and wiring buses. The power

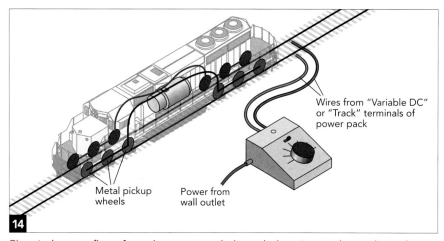

14 Electrical power flows from the power pack through the wires to the track. At the track, electrons flow from one rail through the wheels to the motor and then back to the power pack following the opposite rail.

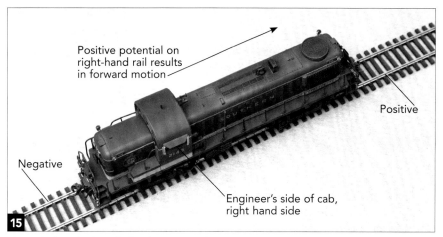

15 The right-hand rule calls for the electrical pathway to be designed so that when positive current is connected to the right-hand track and the locomotive is facing forward, it will move in the forward direction. The long hood on this engine is the front.

supply is usually an AC transformer with a voltage and amperage slightly higher than that of the desired output of the DCC system. Some systems include a power supply, but most do not—many third-party manufacturers offer them.

The *command station*, **8**, is basically the brains of the operation. It keeps track of all the locomotives and accessories in use, the status of the lights, sounds, and any other functions, and it generates the digital signals that are sent out to control all of these. *Boosters*, **9**, take the AC power and convert it into DCC track power, embedding the digital signal from the command station into the power. (Some command stations have a built-in booster.)

Throttles (also called *cabs*), **10**, serve two purposes: They allow you to interact with the command station and they allow you to control locomotives and certain accessories. Throttles range from simple to complex. Some only allow locomotive selection and speed/direction control; others look like small hand-held computers, with multiple buttons for controlling lights, sounds, and other functions.

Decoders come in two varieties, mobile and stationary. Mobile decoders, **11**, are the small electronic devices installed in locomotives that decode

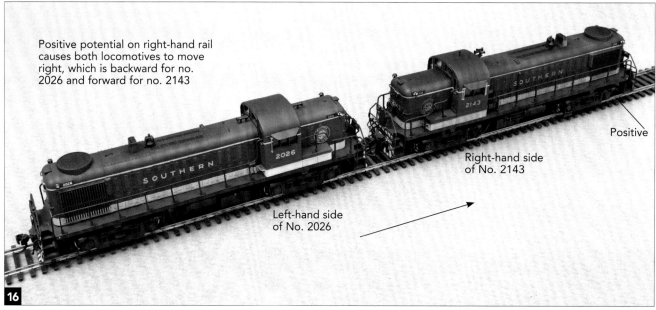

16 A byproduct of the right-hand rule is that when two locomotives are placed on the track facing in opposite directions they will still move in the same direction when power is applied.

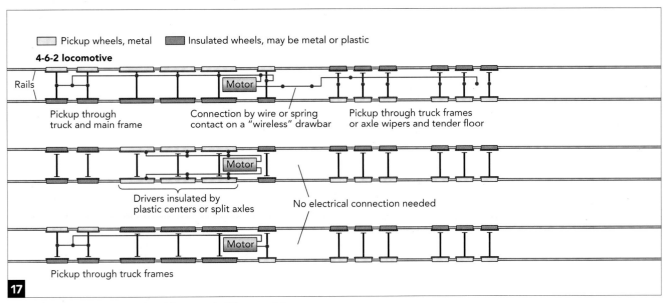

17

Steam locomotives are made with several different pickup arrangements.

the digital signal from the command station, convert track power into DC power to control locomotive speed and direction, turn lights and other functions on and off, and in some cases provide prototype sound output. Stationary decoders, **12**, take track power, decode the signal, and use it to control switch machines, lights, and any other accessory that is electrically operated.

Wires and buses

There's a lot more to wiring a model railroad than just hooking up a couple wires to the track. Wires serve a number of purposes on a layout. A set of wires dedicated to a specific purpose are called a bus. The most obvious of these are the wires from the power pack (or booster, for DCC) to the track, which is called a *power bus*.

There are also wires that power and control turnouts, signals, occupancy detectors, and other accessories. If you use plug-in walkaround throttles you will need a throttle or cab bus. Some advanced modelers even provide their layouts with varying degrees of computer control, which may require very specialized wiring.

Installing all of this wiring in a manner that guarantees the layout will not only work, but also be easy to troubleshoot and maintain, can be a logistical and technical challenge. There are many products on the

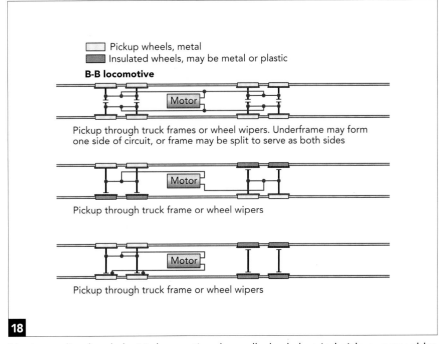

18

Most new diesel and electric locomotives have all-wheel electrical pickup; many older models only pick up power from two wheels on each side.

market today that can streamline this task, and this book will guide you through the process.

Track

Over the 200-plus years of railroad history, track has evolved along with the locomotives and rolling stock. Early track consisting of iron straps attached to wooden stringers was soon replaced with iron rails having a roughly I-shaped cross section. Steel rails were next, and as trains got bigger

and heavier so did the rails.

Consequently, model track is available in a variety of sizes including code 55, 70, 83, and 100, corresponding to progressively larger prototype rails, **13**. The code numbers refer to the height of the rail in thousandths of an inch, so code 83 is .083" tall. As chapter 10 explains, this difference in size has consequences with respect to the electrical conductance of the rails and the way we wire them.

For many years code 100 was the

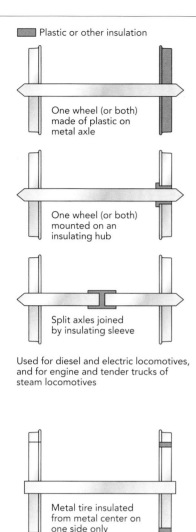

■ Plastic or other insulation

One wheel (or both) made of plastic on metal axle

One wheel (or both) mounted on an insulating hub

Split axles joined by insulating sleeve

Used for diesel and electric locomotives, and for engine and tender trucks of steam locomotives

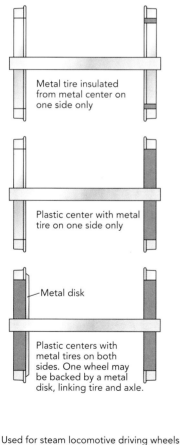

Metal tire insulated from metal center on one side only

Plastic center with metal tire on one side only

Metal disk

Plastic centers with metal tires on both sides. One wheel may be backed by a metal disk, linking tire and axle.

Used for steam locomotive driving wheels

19

Locomotives use several methods for insulating wheels.

most popular HO track, due in part to the deep wheel flanges on early rolling stock. However, code 100 track is oversized for representing all but the heaviest track used by prototype railroads. By the 1990s, code 83 track increasingly replaced code 100 in popularity. Similarly in N scale, code 80 rail has been giving way to more-prototypical code 55 rail.

Because railroads use lighter rail on sidings, spurs, and branch lines, many modelers now vary rail sizes on their layouts. For example, I use code 83 track for my main line and code 70 track on my industrial spurs.

In addition to the variety of sizes, track has also been available with rail of different materials including brass, nickel silver, and steel. Through the 1970s, brass was the most popular material for rail, but its popularity has declined over the past few decades due its unprototypical color and other issues. Brass is highly conductive but the oxide coating that forms atop brass rail is not, so keeping brass track clean can be a nagging maintenance issue.

Nickel silver has become the most popular material for model rail. Nickel silver, an alloy containing copper, zinc, and nickel (but no silver) does not conduct electricity as well as brass. However, the oxide coating that develops on nickel silver rail is conductive, so it is easier to maintain. It wears well and has a prototypically accurate color for the railhead. It is available in all common sizes and scales and in a wide variety of turnouts, crossings, and crossovers.

Steel track is available mainly in train sets. It can rust if not regularly cleaned. It is difficult to cut and shape, and it can't be soldered with a conventional iron. Most modelers avoid it for permanent layouts.

Consequently, unless you have a large collection of older brass code 100 track that has been given to you—and even then you may want to reconsider—you will most likely use nickel silver track.

Locomotives

Locomotive construction and assembly varies among models, but all have common components and operate in a similar manner. Let's start at the bottom.

The wheels pick up power from the rails. Most models today feature all-wheel electrical pickup; on some older models and newer low-quality models, only two wheels on each truck (or one side of the drivers on a steam locomotive) pick up electricity.

The wheels on each side of the locomotive pass electricity to the motor, sometimes via the truck frame or metal chassis and/or separate wires or a circuit board. In any case, the motor has two electrical connections: one to each rail.

Electricity flows from the power pack through wires to the track. At the track, current flows through the wheels along one rail to the motor and then back to the wheels on the opposite side to the track and back to the power pack, **14**. With a DCC system the circuit is essentially the same, with the addition of a decoder positioned in the pathway before the motor.

Many years ago the NMRA adopted standard S9, the right-hand rule, to guarantee that all locomotives operate in a predictable direction. This rule calls for the electrical pathway to be designed so that when a positive potential is connected to the right-hand track and the locomotive is facing forward (with the engineer's side of the cab on the right hand side), it will move in the forward direction, **15**. This is a very convenient arrangement since it means that if a pair of locomotives is placed on the track facing opposite directions, they will still move in the same direction when power is applied, **16**. This is simplified with DCC control because direction of travel is controlled by the command station and decoder.

Although standard S9 established the right hand rule, it did not specify how it is to be achieved. Consequently manufacturers have approached it with different methods for steam, **17**, and diesel, **18**, locomotives. The method that uses the greatest number of wheels for electrical pickup will give the best locomotive performance.

On older steam locomotives it was

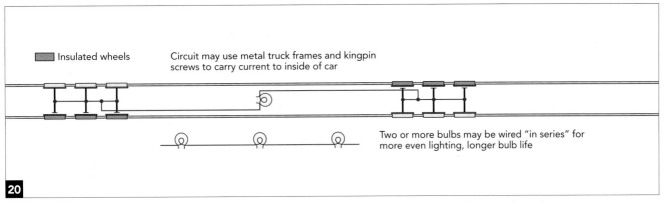

Circuit may use metal truck frames and kingpin screws to carry current to inside of car

Two or more bulbs may be wired "in series" for more even lighting, longer bulb life

20

Here's the usual method for illuminated rolling stock to pick up power using opposing wheels on each truck.

Common motors include (from left) open-frame, can, and flat can.

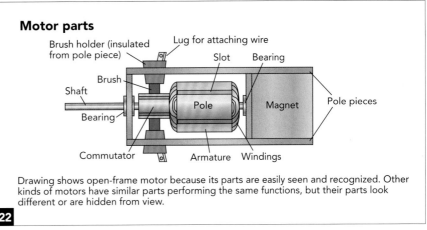

Motor parts

Brush holder (insulated from pole piece)

Lug for attaching wire

Slot

Bearing

Brush

Shaft

Pole

Magnet

Pole pieces

Bearing

Commutator

Armature

Windings

Drawing shows open-frame motor because its parts are easily seen and recognized. Other kinds of motors have similar parts performing the same functions, but their parts look different or are hidden from view.

22

Here are the components of an open-frame motor.

common practice for the wheels on the right side of the locomotive to pick up from the right rail while the wheels on the left side of the tender picked up from the left rail. Obviously this arrangement required an electrical connection between the locomotive and the tender, which could be unreliable. On some modern steam models the wheels on both sides of the locomotive pick up power and the tender wheels are not used at all. The most modern and efficient form is to have the wheels on both sides of the locomotive and tender pick up power.

Diesel locomotive models followed a similar evolution in design, with early models having one truck's wheels pick up from the right rail and the other truck's wheels pick up power from the left rail. Currently the most common method is to have all the wheels on each side to pick up power from their respective rails.

The wheels on each locomotive axle must be insulated from one another to

prevent short circuits. On diesel models this can be accomplished by using one insulated wheel on one side or by splitting the axle and joining it with a nonconductive connector, **19**. On steam models the metal tire may be insulated from the center of the driver, or the center itself may be nonconductive material. Another approach is to use plastic centers on both wheels. On some locomotives, metal wheel wipers then transfer electrical power from the metal portions of the wheels to wires going to the motor.

Similar approaches to those just described are used for lighted rolling stock such as passenger cars and cabooses. For example, the wheels on one truck may pick up from the right rail while those on the other truck pick up power only from the left rail, **20**. Another more efficient method is to have both wheels on both trucks pick up power from both rails. The first method can result in flickering lights whereas the second is much more reliable.

Motors

Motor technology has come a long way in the last 100 years. There are three basic motor types: open-frame, can (enclosed), and coreless, **21**.

The open-frame motor, **22**, was the standard of the model railroad industry for decades but now is seldom used in models. These consist of a permanent magnet at one end of the motor with two metal plates extending forward from it. These metal plates are oriented so that one carries the north magnetic field and other the south magnetic field.

Between these magnetic plates sits the armature, which forms the rotating electromagnet. This is constructed of metal plates set on a metal shaft with insulated copper wire wound around them. The ends of the copper wires are attached to metal plates on the shaft called commutators. There is one commutator for each pole of the motor and they are separated by a small space. The brushes are carbon blocks that rub against the commutators and transmit DC power to them.

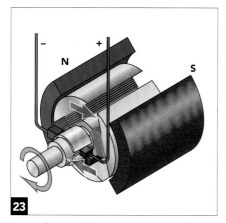 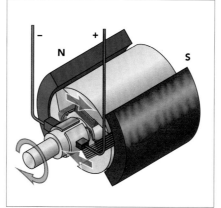 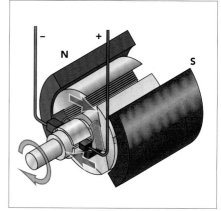

Here's how a DC motor operates. When current is applied, the two poles of the motor windings—having opposite polarities—are drawn toward their opposite poles on the permanent magnet and away from their like poles (left). As the armature rotates, the poles of the motor are now in line with their opposite poles on the permanent magnet—note the commutator is about to switch from the negative brush to the positive brush (center). Once the commutator passes to the positive brush, the electromagnetic field reverses (right). This renews the attraction/repulsion action and maintain rotation.

When DC electricity is applied, it passes through the brushes to the commutators and from there to the wire windings, creating an electromagnetic field, **23**. Because the electromagnetic field sits between the north and south magnetic poles of the permanent magnet, it rotates when power is applied. This rotation occurs because the electromagnetic north pole is attracted to the south pole and repulsed by the north pole of the permanent magnet. This same but opposite action occurs at the south pole of the electromagnet. As the armature rotates, each commutator in turn comes into contact with the brushes, causing the electromagnetic field on each pole of the motor to reverse, maintaining the rotation.

Can motors are more efficient versions of the basic open-frame motor, with semicircular permanent magnets placed around the electromagnet. The flat can motor has permanent magnets that do not completely encircle the armature. Compared to an equivalent open-frame motor, a can motor generally begins to turn at a much lower voltage and draws less current. For example, an older open-frame motor in an HO engine might require 1A or more at full speed, but a modern can motor may only require .3-.5A. Can motors also tend to operate more smoothly with greater torque. One reason for this improved performance has been the change in the number and shape of the armature poles.

The first motors used by Carlisle and Finch had only two poles. This caused an effect called "cogging" at slow speeds, because the motor hesitated briefly as the electromagnetic field reversed. Increasing the number of poles to three and later five smoothed out cogging and increased torque. Another development that resulted in smoother performance was skewing the armature plates and windings, **24**. Most locomotive models produced today have five-pole, skew-wound motors.

Although uncommon, some manufacturers have used coreless motors in model locomotives. Externally these look the same as can motors, but they have a different internal configuration. As the name implies, coreless motors have windings without the metal armature plates. These motors are very efficient and draw even less current than a can motor. However, because they lack the metal armature they may not be as efficient at dissipating heat.

Motors are designed to operate safely at certain amperage levels. Above these levels they may begin to overheat, leading to partial melting of the insulating layer on the windings and a short circuit in the motor. Consequently it is not a good idea to overload locomotives. If you notice that the motor in one is running hot, check its current draw. I'll discuss how to measure current draw in Chapter 13. If the motor is drawing too much current, it may burn out.

The motor on the top locomotive model has straight armature plates and windings, whereas those on the bottom are skewed.

Jeff Wilson

CHAPTER TWO

Traditional DC power

Early model railroaders had to jump through hoops to get DC power to operate their locomotives. However, by the 1930s a number of advances in electronics started to change this. First came the step-down transformer, which could drop AC power down to safe voltage and current, **1**. Next came the rectifier, a device that could convert AC to DC. Put the two together and you had a workable power supply for scale model locomotives.

Today's modern transistorized power packs, such as this MRC Tech 7, offer outstanding speed control and performance for standard DC layouts compared to older rheostat-controlled models.

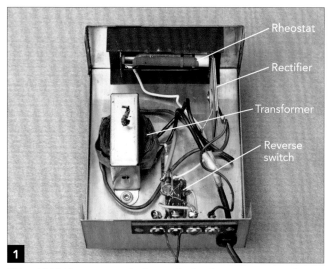

1 This old MRC power pack shows the basic components of a non-transistorized, rheostat-controlled power pack. The transformer drops the incoming 120VAC power to safe voltage and amperage levels at 18VDC at less than one amp.

Labels (image 1): Rheostat, Rectifier, Transformer, Reverse switch

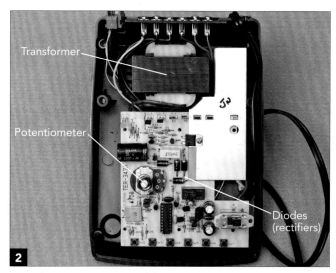

2 A modern MRC power pack has a much larger transformer, a potentiometer for improved speed control, four silicon diodes forming a rectifier, a filter capacitor, and sophisticated transistorized electronics.

Labels (image 2): Transformer, Potentiometer, Diodes (rectifiers)

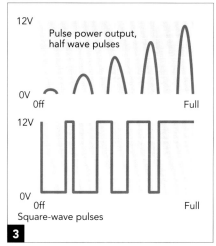

3 Pulse power provides an added kick to the motor to help fine-tune slow-speed operations. At bottom, square waves produced by silicon-controlled rectifiers (SCRs) can also smooth low-speed operation.

Labels (image 3): 12V, Pulse power output, half wave pulses, 0V, Off, Full, 12V, 0V, Off, Full, Square-wave pulses

Power packs

A *power pack* is the term for a sealed unit that combines the transformer, rectifier, and speed/directional controls. Power packs feature DC output for trains—distinguished from toy train controllers that have AC output, which are commonly called *transformers*.

Power packs have knobs or dials to control the voltage sent to the tracks. Into the 1980s, this was generally done with a *rheostat*, which is made of a single strand of wire wound around ceramic or other nonconductive material. A sliding metal contact moved along the wire winding, completing the circuit. Because the small wire resists the flow of electrons, the position of the metal slider along it determines the output voltage.

Power packs today use *potentiometers* to control speed. Potentiometers are similar to rheostats but instead of a wire resistor they employ carbon or cermet (ceramic/metal) for the resistive element, **2**. A wiper moved along the resistive element varies the output voltage, usually by controlling a power transistor. The result is finer voltage control and smoother locomotive operation.

Power packs are sometimes referred to as throttles, but that term really refers only to the potentiometer and its associated circuitry. Consequently you could have a throttle separate from the transformer and rectifier that make up the basic power supply.

In addition to controlling track voltage, power packs often have additional features such as accessory power outlets, pulse power, momentum features, brakes, and programmability.

Before we look at these additional features, let me toss out a warning against buying older power packs at train shows, flea markets, and internet auction sites. Although older rheostat-equipped packs may have been adequate to operate the higher-amperage motors common through the 1980s, they're not a good choice for modern, efficient can motors. In fact, many newer motors are so efficient that they don't generate a large enough electrical load for the rheostat to be able to control their speed.

Another factor to consider is that Z and N scale locomotive motors have a lower maximum safe operating voltage than HO scale, and many old power packs may exceed that. For example, motors for Z scale locomotives should not be operated with more than 8VDC. To address this issue, MRC offers the AT880 voltage reducer that will drop the voltage by about four volts. **Bottom line:** *If you are pondering picking up a used power pack, make sure you know what you're getting before you buy.*

Pulse power

A few decades ago it was observed that it is possible to achieve better low-speed control using pulse power. Pulse power is just what it sounds like: small pulses of electricity are either added onto the DC power or the entire DC output may be in pulses, **3**. The pulses basically give a little extra kick to the motor at slow speeds and thus help overcome the effects of cogging and friction. As motor speed increases, the pulses have little effect

4

Some power packs, like this MRC model, offer momentum and brake effects for advanced locomotive operation.

5

Screw terminals provide handy connections between the power pack and the track and accessories.

and may be automatically cut off by the power pack circuitry. This is especially desirable since some pulse power can actually cause a motor to heat up, and as we know from Chapter 1, heat is not a good thing. Pulse power was more beneficial for older open-frame motors—modern motors generally run fine at low speeds.

Another type of pulse power can be generated using silicon-controlled rectifiers (SCRs), which create square wave pulses at a full 12VDC, **3**. This type of circuit works by controlling how long the pulse power, and therefore the motor, is on and off. A series of short-duration (full-voltage) square-wave pulses means the motor is on less of the time and the speed will be slower. If the pulses are on for longer durations then the speed will increase. SCR throttle designs were very popular among modelers who built their own throttles during the 1970s, and they were found in some commercial products as well.

Momentum and brakes

Due to the great weight of the trains they are pulling, prototype locomotives can't rapidly speed up or slow down. To replicate this action, some power packs offer a feature called *momentum*, **4**. This feature (which usually has an on-off switch) gradually increases and decreases the voltage to the throttle setting, so the locomotive speed increases or decreases slowly as if it were pulling a heavy string of cars.

A related feature on some power packs is *braking*. This allows you to

reduce locomotive power in small increments, giving you much finer control over locomotive speed than might be accomplished using the throttle alone. Braking is usually controlled by a spring-loaded slide or toggle switch, or by a pressure-sensitive push button.

Accessory power

Modelers often install lights, signals, and other animated devices on their layouts, all requiring power. Some power packs have both constant DC and AC screw terminals in addition to the variable DC terminals to provide power for these accessories, **5**. This power usually is around 18VAC and 16VDC, so you may have to use dropping resistors or diodes to reduce this voltage to the 12 volts required by many accessories.

The downside to using accessory terminals is that the power used is then not available to operate your trains, so you need to plan for that when choosing a power pack. Also, depending on the electronics of the power pack the output voltage may decrease as the load is increased—in other words, it may not be regulated. Consequently, if you plan to use a lot of accessories on your layout it is usually better to install a dedicated power supply with a regulated voltage output. We'll look at accessory power in more detail in Chapter 13.

Walkaround throttles

Through the mid-1960s the accepted practice for operating most model

6

MRC offers this walkaround throttle that can be added to its Throttlepack 9900 and 9950 and Tech 6 Sound Controller systems.

railroads was to place all the controls in one location, with the engineers sitting or standing at the controls and watching as their trains traversed the layout. However, beginning in the mid-1960s Allen McClelland changed all that when he popularized handheld walkaround controls on his HO scale Virginian & Ohio layout. Although Allen used an early type of analog command control, many modelers built hand-held DC throttles that could be plugged into a power bus as they walked around the layout with their trains.

Into the 1980s and 1990s, some manufacturers took the hint and offered them as well, but I could only find a handful still in production including one for the MRC Throttlepack 9900 and 9950, the Tech

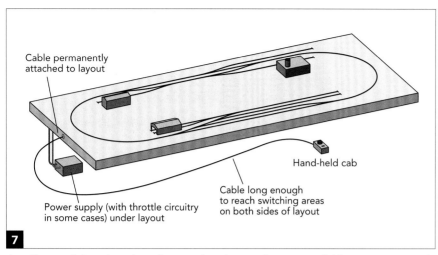

Cable permanently attached to layout

Hand-held cab

Power supply (with throttle circuitry in some cases) under layout

Cable long enough to reach switching areas on both sides of layout

7

A walkaround throttle tethered to one location can be very useful for operating yards and on small layouts.

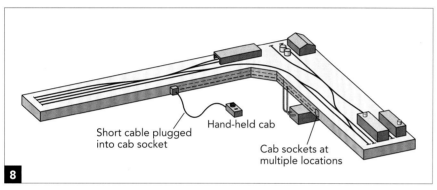

Short cable plugged into cab socket

Hand-held cab

Cab sockets at multiple locations

8

For larger around-the-walls or island-style layouts you'll need a way to move your throttle as you walk along with your train. Installing several sockets daisy-chained with a power and control bus allows easily moving a throttle.

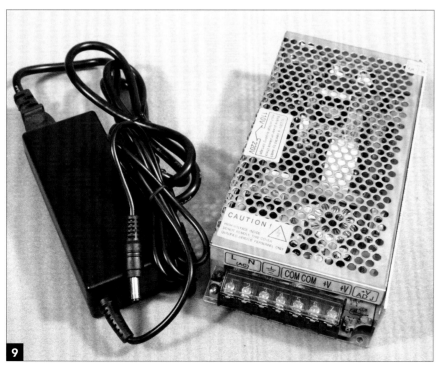

9

Power supplies that plug directly into a wall outlet are available in many voltage and amperage ratings.

6 Sound Controller, **6**, and the Dallee Engineer and Yardmaster.

When considering a walkaround throttle there are several options to keep in mind. On small layouts it may be easier to use a tethered throttle that is permanently wired to one central location with a long cable, **7**. Although a good option for a small switching layout, this arrangement may become cumbersome if you need to operate on the opposite side of a large island-type layout. In most cases it is best to install several sockets around your layout where the throttle can be plugged in as you follow your train, **8**. Another useful addition to walkaround throttles is memory. This feature allows a locomotive to keep running at its set speed even when the throttle is unplugged.

The limited availability of commercial walkaround throttles for DC operations shouldn't stop you from building your own. Many articles and plans for walkaround throttles have appeared in the pages of *Model Railroader* and other magazines, ranging from basic designs to those including momentum, braking, and memory. There are also many circuits available on various websites, so try an internet search. One example is a simple transistorized throttle that was published in the January 1986 *Model Railroader*. All the parts are still available from suppliers like All Electronics, Digi-Key, Jameco, Mouser, and Radio Shack.

To power a separate throttle (commercial or home-built), the best option is to pick up a DC power supply, **9**, from one of the electrical parts suppliers listed in the Appendix. These power supplies are available in various voltage and amperage ratings.

How much power?

Power packs are available in several amperage ratings ranging from less than one amp (including many small power packs included with train sets) to more than two amps. How do you decide what your needs are?

First, consider the locomotives and scale. As explained in Chapter 1, motors have changed a lot over the last

Locomotives with headlight 1.0A	Passenger cars with two bulbs each .03A x 2 = .06A	.06A	.06A	.06A	.06A

Locomotive current 1.0A
Car light current 5 x 0.06A = 0.3A
Total current for train: 1.3A

10

The lighted cars in a passenger train may require almost as much current as the locomotive. The total power draw needs to be considered when choosing a power supply or power pack.

30 years and the amount of current they require has decreased greatly. Consequently if you have a collection of older locomotives, they may require as much as 1 to 1.5 amps each! Modern HO locomotives, on the other hand, typically require .3 to .5 amps, and smaller N and Z scale models usually draw even less current.

Just because a locomotive only draws .3 amps doesn't necessarily mean you can get away with buying a .5-amp power pack, especially if you are operating diesel locomotives. While steam locomotives typically run by themselves, diesels are usually run in multiple-unit consists. So, if you want to operate a two- or three-unit consist, you'll need a power pack with enough power to run all of them at the same time. Another factor to consider is that if there are any other powered accessories in the train such as a sound unit or lighted cars, then the power demands of those have to be added into the total power needs.

Let's look at an example of a five car passenger train pulled by a pair of diesel locomotives with sound unit installed, **10**. Assuming these are fairly new locomotives they probably have very efficient can motors requiring less than 0.5A each at maximum load with sound and lights turned on. Next consider that the five cars are each lighted with two incandescent bulbs that draw 30mA (.03A) each. Add that all up and we find that a power pack capable of supplying 1.3 amps would be required. Now if you also wanted to hook up interior lights for the station and stores in town along with some other accessories, you could end up needing a 2A power pack.

How do you know the amperage output of a power pack? Although

11
Deltang is a British system using a small battery and receiver/controller to operate locomotives without powering the track. *Geren Mortensen*

many will state it outright in their advertising, on the box, and on the unit itself, there is an easy way to check. The output capacities are usually printed on the power pack case near the screw terminals, **5**. Look for the total output in volt-amps (VA). Dividing this value by 12 (volts) you will know the output amperage. For example, a 16VA power pack will deliver about 1.3 amps.

Going wireless

Many articles have appeared in the hobby press detailing how to build wireless walkaround throttles. Aristo-Craft manufactured the Train Engineer wireless throttle, which was popular with both large scale modelers and N scale modular clubs. However, Aristo-Craft ceased operations in 2013.

More recently, large scale modelers have been installing batteries in their locomotives and operating them using wireless throttles, eliminating the need to power the track. With continued miniaturization, batteries and receiver/controllers are now available that will fit inside O scale locomotives and some HO locomotive tenders. One example is the Deltang system from the UK, **11**. Eventually I expect these systems will be small enough to fit in a powered HO diesel loco, although for now a dummy unit holding the battery and receiver/controller could be mated with a powered unit. Even if we do manage to eliminate the need for power on the track, we'll still have to run wires for all the turnouts and accessories, so don't throw out your soldering iron and wire cutters yet.

Jeff Wilson

CHAPTER THREE

Digital Command Control (DCC) basics

Digital Command Control systems have become more popular in recent years. Many locomotive models are now available with built-in decoders, making the transition to DCC easier than ever.

Command control systems have been around since the early 1960s. The value of command control is it allows multiple operators to independently control several locomotives on the same piece of track using small receivers or decoders installed in each locomotive. The command control signal is embedded in the electric power supplied to the track, **1**, and each decoder reads that information and acts upon the commands programmed into it.

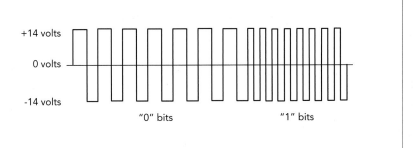

1

DCC track power is a type of alternating current, but with square waves instead of curved sine waves. In this example it is constantly fluctuating between positive 14V and negative 14V. The width of the square waves is varied to produce both wide and narrow forms to create the "0" and "1" bits which make up the bits and bytes of the digital signal. Normally the frequency of the waves is too fast for DC motors to respond, but some manufacturers stretch the "0" bit by keeping it on long enough to actually power a locomotive without a decoder.

Most entry-level DCC systems (this is Bachmann's E-Z Command) can only control and power a few locomotives.

3

More-advanced DCC systems typically have enough memory for dozens of locomotives and provide power for 10 to 20 locomotives.

4

Many boosters have a switch or other means of controlling their output voltage.

5

Either an AC or DC power supply is required for each booster. Most manufacturers offer one suitable for their systems.

These commands allow the decoder to control a number of functions including speed, direction, lights, and sound. The decoder essentially acts as a miniature power pack, converting track power to DC and feeding it to the motor.

Why command control

As you'll see in Chapter 5, operating two or more trains at a time using standard DC power packs can get very complicated very fast. The really important aspect of command control is that even on small layouts you can independently operate a larger number of locomotives without a lot of extensive wiring, so it greatly simplifies the wiring and control process.

Early command control systems, such as Dynatrol and CTC-16, were proprietary. Each manufacturer's system had its own protocol and only worked with its own receivers and components. With DCC, manufacturers follow

the same protocol, allowing decoders from one company to be controlled by another's system. The method the DCC signal is sent (pulse-width modulation—more on that in a bit) is more reliable, and the two-way communication of DCC—decoders can "talk back" to the command station—also enables more system and decoder features.

DCC opens up a whole new world of accessories and special functions for your locomotives. Decoders offer the ability to control headlights, classification lights, ditch lights, Mars (rotating signal) lights, rooftop strobe lights or beacons, horns, bells, whistles, steam chuff, prime mover, and numerous other sounds in your locomotives. Throttle-controlled accessory decoders can control turnouts and just about any other device you would normally power using a DC power supply. Let's take a more detailed look at the various components of a DCC system.

Command stations

The command station is essentially the brains of a DCC system. It creates the command signal that is sent to locomotives and accessory decoders. In addition, command stations keep track of the status of all the functions for your various decoders and regularly update the commands sent to them, including locomotive speed, whether lights should be on or off, direction of travel, and even which locomotives are part of a multi-unit consist.

You'll use the command station when you program your decoders. The command station also acts as the interface between your DCC system and a computer if you choose to add that capability.

Command stations vary in their capabilities. Some entry-level command stations, **2**, may only be able to keep track of a handful of locomotives whereas more advanced models, **3**, have enough memory to keep track of more

Throttles can vary from very simple units having little more than a control knob and a few control buttons to large devices resembling a handheld computer.

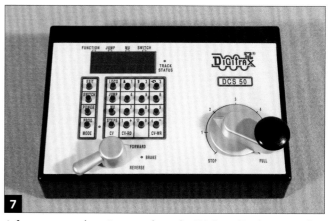

A few command stations, such as the Digitrax Zephyr, actually have a throttle or two built into them. These are usually aimed at the new-user or small-layout market.

than a hundred. However, that doesn't mean you can actually operate that many simultaneously since you are still limited by the total amperage output of your DCC system.

Most command stations also contain a booster to provide power to operate trains (more on those in a bit). However, a few systems are available with just the command station alone. The advantage of the combination units is you only have to buy the one component. However. if the booster circuitry dies, then you may need to replace the whole unit. That said, some of my systems are 20 years old and have never been back to the manufacturer for repair. Also, with the separate command station approach, you can select whatever amperage booster you may need.

Boosters

The control signal created by the command station needs to be increased to the full operating voltage and amperage required to operate your locomotives—that's where the booster comes in. As its name implies, the booster takes the command signal and boosts it to about 12 volts for N scale, 14 volts for HO, and 18-22 volts for O and larger scales (these values may vary depending on manufacturer designs). Some designs have a switch allowing you to select the voltage range for your layout and some have internal controls that allow you to fine-tune the voltage, **4**. Be aware that some introductory systems simply put out a

voltage proportional to what you feed in, dropping it by only a couple of volts.

Boosters are available with ratings ranging from 2 to 10 amps, and you can use multiple boosters to power different sections of your layout. In choosing a booster, it's critical to know how much power your layout requires. Some modelers mistakenly assume it is a good idea to use one 10A booster instead of two 5A units. However, a 10A booster running at 14 volts is putting out 140 watts, which in case of a sustained short circuit can create enough heat to melt N scale locomotive sideframes and potentially weld wheels to rails. One manufacturer told me that under a sustained short his 10 amp booster melted code 70 rail! Chapter 6 explains DCC layout wiring in more detail, including instructions on how to use large-amperage boosters and share the power among several blocks safely.

Boosters come with built-in short-circuit protection and they shut down when a short occurs. That means that every train in the block powered by that booster will also shut down until the short is cleared. As you will see in Chapter 6, you can add additional boosters in separate blocks to limit the effects of short circuits, or you can install multiple circuit breakers between the booster and the track. Several manufacturers also offer stand-alone circuit breakers that make it easy to add additional protection and help manage your power needs on medium to large layouts.

Locating command stations and boosters

The various components in a DCC system mean you have some choices regarding how they go together and where to put them. There are two types of connections between the command station and boosters: the command bus and a ground line. The command bus consists of the wires that carry the command signal from the command station to the boosters. This bus is usually daisy-chained among multiple boosters. Some manufacturers also recommend that a large diameter ground wire be connected between the command station and boosters.

Locating the boosters next to one another greatly reduces the length of the command bus and ground lines, simplifying your wiring. This arrangement also makes it easier to troubleshoot a problem and to keep boosters cool (more on that in Chapter 13). However, there are instances where distributing your boosters around the layout should be considered—more on that in Chapter 6.

Powering a DCC system

Providing power to your command station and boosters requires an AC or DC power supply, **5**. It is recommended that you have a separate power supply for each booster. Most manufacturers offer suitable units compatible with their systems. Some additional manufacturers and suppliers also offer compatible units (see Appendix B).

The power supply should match the booster's output ratings. In most cases an old DC power pack will not provide enough amperage to operate your booster. For example, a 5A booster to be used with HO locomotives at about 14 volts would require a power supply rated at about 5A and 16V. The extra two volts covers the voltage drop due to internal circuitry. Any extra voltage above that will have to dissipated as heat, which can contribute to heat buildup in your booster and increase the likelihood of thermal shutdowns. If in doubt, follow the manufacturer's recommendations.

It might seem like it would be an easy task to simply plug in a power supply, hook it up to your booster, and run trains. Although this is fairly accurate for a small layout, for a medium- to large-sized layout there are other factors to consider. First, you'll likely need a 5A supply for each command station/booster. The good news is that a 5A power supply doesn't require anywhere near 5 amps from the household supply. For example, a 16VAC, 5A supply would only pull between .67 and 1.0 amps. However, you will need extra capacity to power other devices, and many basement circuits also power room lights, garage doors, dehumidifiers, etc. Unless you have multiple circuits in your train room, that means you may be limited in the number of command stations, boosters, and other equipment you can safely operate.

Most household electrical circuits for wall outlets are rated at 15 amps, and according to building codes these should not carry a sustained load of more than about 80 percent of that rating, or about 12 amps. So if you are going to be building even a moderate-sized layout, plan ahead and do some quick estimates of how much power you will need. Just to be safe, in addition to the original 15A circuit in my train room, I have a 20A circuit dedicated to powering my overhead lighting. In Chapter 6 I'll also give you some tips on how to use power management to reduce the number of boosters you actually need to operate a layout.

8 Mobile decoders are available in a large variety of amperage ratings with varying numbers of functions and additional features.

9 It is now common for decoders to be designed as drop-in replacements for the light/wiring board in locomotives, making them very easy to install.

Throttles

Throttles (or cabs) are the devices that allow you to communicate with the command station and to control your locomotives and other devices. These can vary from very simple units having little more than a control knob and a few control buttons to large devices with many function buttons, **6**.

There are wireless throttles that use infrared emitters and receivers, as well as those using radio. The radio-control cabs are available in versions that only send signals to the command station as well as units capable of two-way communications.

A few command stations have a throttle or two built into them—these are usually aimed at the new-user market, **7**.

Since the throttle is the one device that you will be using more than any other, it's a good idea to pick a system with throttles you are comfortable with, both physically and operationally.

Decoders

Decoders take the incoming DCC signal and turn it to action by powering locomotive motors and headlights, switch machines, and other accessories. There are two types of decoders: *mobile* (locomotive) and *stationary*.

Mobile decoders are available in a wide variety of amperage ratings and functions, **8**. There are many decoders

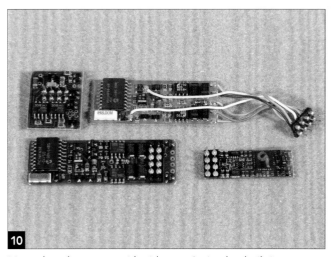

10

Many decoders come with either an 8-pin plug built into them or have the 8-pin plug attached via wires. These can be plugged into a socket mounted in the locomotive.

11

Another popular option is a plastic female socket built into the end of the decoder which can be attached to wires or a compatible male socket in a locomotive.

designed for specific locomotives in Z, N, HO, and O scales, making them very easy to install. This is especially important when it comes to installing a sound-equipped decoder. These decoders usually are a drop-in replacement for the light board in the locomotive, **9**.

Generic decoders usually come with either an 8-pin plug built into them or have the 8-pin plug attached via wires, **10**. Another popular option is a plastic female socket built into the end of the decoder which can be attached to

wires or a compatible male socket in a locomotive, **11**. Although some of these are called "plug and play," you still usually have to connect headlights and a speaker to the decoder. Chapter 13 shows a basic decoder installation.

Stationary decoders are mainly used for controlling switch machines. They are also available with a range of options, **12**. Some are designed to operate specific switch machines such as the Tortoise slow-motion (stall motor), solenoid-based "snap" machines, and Kato's Unitrak switch

machines, whereas others can power and control all types.

Some stationary decoders can also be used to control layout lighting and other accessories as long as the accessories do not exceed the output capacity of the unit. Most are powered directly using track power, but some allow for a separate power supply—more on those in Chapter 13.

Programming decoders

Programming is the process of setting the address and function settings (called *configuration variables* or CVs) in your mobile and stationary decoders. There are two ways to program mobile decoders: service mode and operations (ops) mode. Service-mode programming is accomplished by placing your decoder-equipped locomotive on an electrically isolated section of track. This is necessary because service-mode programming is indiscriminate and will result in reprogramming all locos on this track to the same settings.

No matter which type of system you have, it is necessary to have an isolated section of track in a yard and/or on your workbench where you can do your decoder programming. Some systems have separate connections for track power and programming whereas on others they are combined (usually the less-expensive systems). With these you cannot program decoders while you are running trains

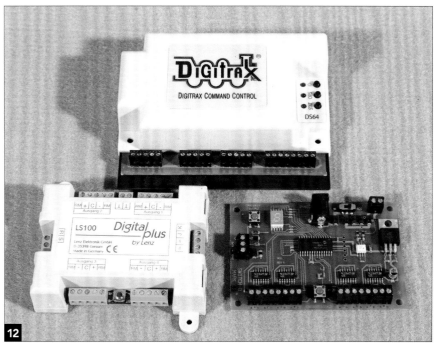

12

Stationary decoders are also available with a range of options that allow you to control switch machines, lights, and other accessories.

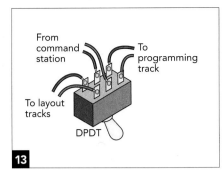

13

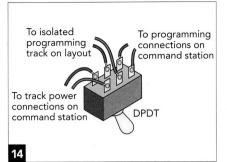

14

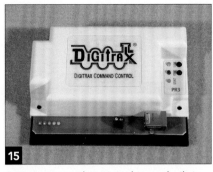

15

Most basic command stations do not support simultaneous locomotive operation and programming. This means you will need to install a DPDT switch to shunt the programming signal to an isolated programming track.

and you need a DPDT switch to isolate the programming track from the main track while programming, **13**. I wired my programming track using a DPDT switch with one pole set for track power and the other set for programming, **14**. I simply run the locomotive to be programmed onto the programming track in my main yard, throw the switch to programming, program the decoder, throw the switch back to track power, and the locomotive is ready to go.

Ops mode programming is done on the main track so it also called "programming on the main." This can be done because the programming commands in ops mode are sent only to a specific decoder based on its address. Ops mode programming is useful for changing just a few settings, for example if you wish to try out different whistle sounds or speed-setting modifications, or if you're trying to speed-match multiple locomotives. However, there are faster ways to handle more complex programming tasks using a computer.

The process for programming accessory decoders can be somewhat different among manufacturers and even among units from the same manufacturer. The ones I'm familiar with initially must be attached directly to track power for programming and cannot be programmed on the programming track. Some have programming jumpers or lockouts that have to be moved or changed to allow programming, which prevents

More advanced command stations have connections for simultaneous operation and programming. On my layout I have a programming track with a DPDT switch that allows a locomotive to be driven onto the programming track. The switch is then thrown to the programming leads. This allows locos to be programmed without removing them from the layout.

inadvertent reprogramming. The good thing is that they can all be used on any DCC system, and once programmed they rarely need reprogramming.

Computer interfaces

Adding a computer to your model railroad may sound like a complicated proposition. However, DCC manufacturers have greatly simplified the task compared to 20 years ago when you almost needed an electronics engineer on your operating crew to handle the job. Most DCC manufacturers now offer a computer interface for their systems, **15**. RR-CirKits produces a number of signal and control devices

Some command stations have a built-in computer interface while others offer stand-alone interfaces like this PR3 from Digitrax.

including their popular LocoBuffer interface for connecting to the Digitrax Loconet system network. RR-CirKits products are designed to integrate with the popular Java Model Railroad Interface (JMRI) freeware. Bruce Chubb's C/MRI system also works with DCC systems and his hardware can also be controlled by JMRI using the interfaces mentioned above.

All these acronyms may sound a bit complicated but what it boils down to is there are a lot of options should you decide to use a computer with your DCC system—but what would you use it for?

One use is to set up a block occupancy and signaling system. Another option is to create a virtual control panel on your computer monitor and use your mouse to align turnouts and set routes for your trains. At the highest level of computer

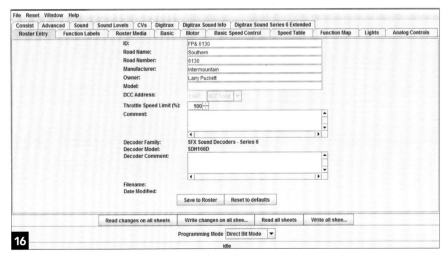

16

DecoderPro is a free program that works with many manufacturer's computer interfaces to program decoders. The graphic interface greatly simplifies programming. Almost all decoders are supported.

operations, you can even automate train movements.

An even more useful feature of computer interfaces is the ability to use the computer to program decoders. For example, the JMRI freeware program *DecoderPro* can program almost any decoder ever made, **16**. And, after programming those decoders you can save the settings to a file in case you ever need to reprogram that decoder again. Plus, once you program one decoder you can use the same settings to program others like it. Programming sound decoders can get pretty complicated, and using using software like DecoderPro can greatly simplify that process. Also, both Digitrax, **15**, and Loksound, **17**, produce interfaces that allow you to download sound packages and install them in their

Some sound decoders can be reprogrammed with new sound packages using interfaces like this one from Loksound.

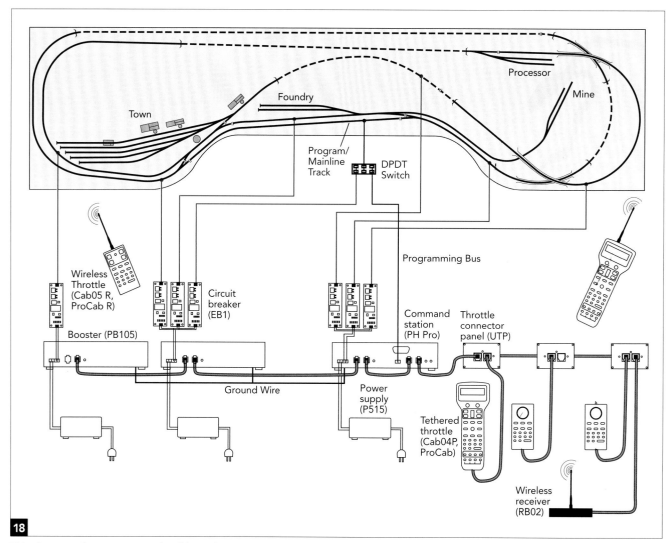

This diagram shows an example of how the components of a typical DCC system are interconnected and wired to the layout, in this case with North Coast Engineering components. *Original diagram courtesy North Coast Engineering*

19

Plastic connectors and flat telephone-type cables are used with most DCC systems to make network and throttle connections.

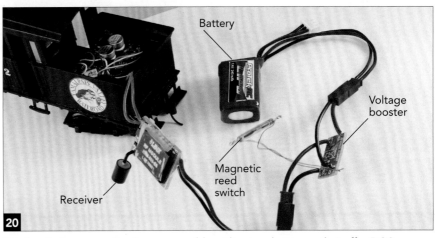

20

Battery

Voltage booster

Magnetic reed switch

Receiver

Totally wireless operation is now possible with several systems that offer DCC compatible transmitters and receivers. The Dead Rail System shown here is made by Tam Valley Depot and includes a transmitter, receiver, and battery pack. *Duncan McCree/Tam Valley Depot*

sound capable decoders. You can even edit and create your own sound packages to customize your sound decoders. I'll provide some more details on computer control in Chapter 12.

Putting it together

Let's look at how all this hardware goes together, **18**. First, you have to wire your power supplies to the command station and boosters to power them. Then you need to add the wires that carry the command signal between the command station and your boosters—this is the *command bus*. You will need another set of wires that snake around your layout for the throttle and accessory bus—the throttle bus or main network. Finally, there are the wires that power the track (track bus) and the programming track. Accessory decoders can receive their power from the track power bus or from a dedicated power bus just for them.

Most systems use flat telephone-type cables (referred to as telco) for the various network connections, **19**. Many accessories such as accessory decoders, throttle connector panels, wireless receivers, computer interfaces, and even boosters are connected to the main network using telco-type cables. Technically there is no difference between the command network and the throttle or cab network—some manufacturers do not distinguish between them whereas others do. Those that do apparently feel that it is better to isolate throttles and other devices—as always, do what your manufacturer recommends.

To see full details of wiring a layout for DCC, turn to Chapter 6.

DC and DCC—an unhappy marriage

I am often asked whether it is possible to mix DC and DCC on the same layout. The answer is "maybe." Some systems allow you to use address "0" to operate one analog locomotive on the layout. However, doing so can cause lag times in the response of DCC operations so I don't recommend it. You can also operate decoder-equipped locomotives with standard DC power if analog conversion is enabled in the decoder. However, if a short occurs on the DCC layout, decoders with this option enabled can run away uncontrollably, so I recommend disabling this option.

Finally, although it is technically possible to have a DC-controlled section of track attached to a DCC track (some modelers try doing this when converting a block-divided DC cab-control layout to DCC), I don't recommend it. If not done properly—or if a locomotive accidentally bridges the rail gaps between the two types of power—you can end up with the voltage of the two systems combined, and decoders and other components can be destroyed.

Going totally wireless

For several years, large-scale modelers have been installing batteries in their locomotives and using wireless throttles to control them. More recently, batteries and system boards have been reduced in size enough to fit into the

tenders of some HO scale steam and larger diesel locomotives. Examples include CVP's miniAirwire900, Stanford's S-cab, and Tam Valley Depot's Dead Rail system. All offer battery power, wireless throttle control, and compatibility with DCC decoders, especially sound decoders.

All of the above systems have a transmitter that sends the DCC signal to a receiver in the locomotive. The receiver is connected to the DCC decoder and a battery, and basically acts as a booster providing the DCC commands and power to operate the locomotive. Each operates in a slightly different manner; the miniAirwire900 and S-cab generate their own DCC signal whereas the Dead Rail system simply transmits the DCC signal generated by a DCC command station, **20**.

The big plus with these systems is avoiding all the issues that come with having power on the rails. Dirty track and short circuits are no longer a problem, which is why garden railroaders were fast to adopt these systems. There are challenges with battery size, recharging, and other issues, but I'm sure that as battery technology advances we'll see them small enough for all HO locomotives. After all, my first CTC-16 receiver was so large that I had to install it in a dummy locomotive coupled to the powered unit. For now, I'll hold onto my soldering irons and wire cutters, but I might just lay some On30 track out in the back yard.

Jeff Wilson

CHAPTER FOUR

Turnouts and crossings

Turnouts—like these on Kalmbach's HO Milwaukee, Racine & Troy club layout—require gapped rails and other special wiring considerations to avoid short circuits.

Scale model trains—the focus of this book—rely on two rails of opposite electrical polarity, while toy-train operators rely on outside rails of the same polarity and a third middle rail of the opposite polarity. Some trolley modelers use a variation of the third-rail method with the overhead wire as the third rail.

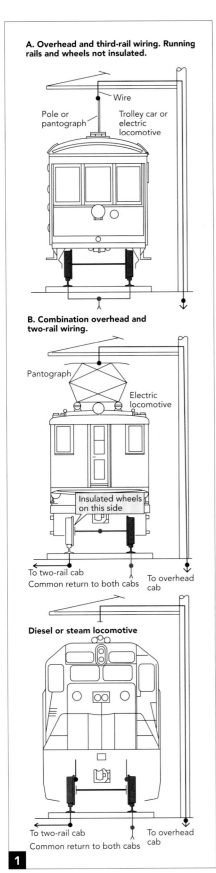

A. Overhead and third-rail wiring. Running rails and wheels not insulated.

Wire

Pole or pantograph

Trolley car or electric locomotive

B. Combination overhead and two-rail wiring.

Pantograph

Electric locomotive

Insulated wheels on this side

To two-rail cab

Common return to both cabs

To overhead cab

Diesel or steam locomotive

To two-rail cab

Common return to both cabs

To overhead cab

1

Wiring for overhead and third-rail operations is fairly straightforward and with a little modification can be combined with two-rail wiring.

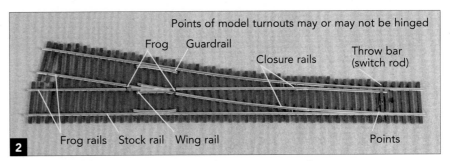

Points of model turnouts may or may not be hinged

Frog   Guardrail

Closure rails

Throw bar (switch rod)

2

Frog rails   Stock rail   Wing rail

Points

This photo illustrates the various parts of a turnout or switch.

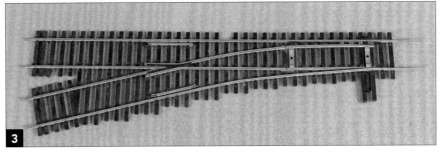

3

Power-routing turnouts like this old Shinohara model direct electricity only to the route selected by the points. Note the metal frog with no gaps between it and the frog rails.

One might think that having only two powered rails would eliminate many wiring issues, but this is not the case! Any time we want our trains to divert from the two rails of the main line to a spur, siding, or adjacent track, we have to use a device called a turnout or switch. Since the two parallel rails are of opposite polarity, the challenge in a turnout is that least one of those two rails must cross the other, creating the possibility of a short circuit. This requires that we follow certain rules in order to avoid these shorts. However, depending upon the type of turnouts used, these practices can create their own issues. Let's take a look at potential problems and how to deal with them.

Turnouts

Let's start by exploring the anatomy of a turnout. As you can see in **2**, there are two continuous outside rails of opposite polarity—these are the *stock rails*. At one end of the turnout are two moveable rails, the *points*, and their *switch rod*, which connects the points to the mechanism that moves them. These parts together form the switch, and this end of the turnout is the point end.

The points are continuous with the *closure rails*, which curve toward and converge at the *frog*—the V-shaped junction where rails of different polarity meet. To avoid potential short circuits at the frog, there are several methods of constructing and wiring turnouts—more on that in a bit. The two rails continuing outward from the frog are the *frog rails*—these make up the diverging tracks leaving the turnout. This is the frog end of a turnout.

Power-routing vs. all-live turnouts

There are two basic types of turnouts: power-routing and all-live (also called *insulated-frog*). Power-routing turnouts, **3**, are designed to route power to whichever route the points are set for, **4**. Power is transferred from the stock rails to the points by physical contact, and from there power is transmitted to the frog and both frog rails by physical contact at joints and through internal wiring. As a consequence of this design, both points/closure rails, the frog, and both frog rails are all the same polarity, which can be both a good and a bad thing.

The good side is that this feature allows you to route power with less trouble—you can selectively power one of the two diverging tracks without additional wiring. This can come in handy should you want to park a locomotive on a spur track and then

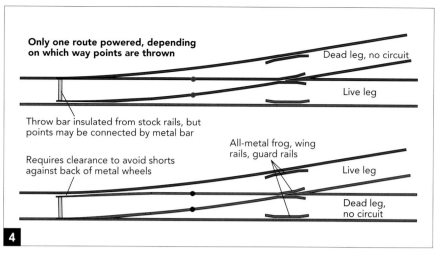

With power-routing turnouts, the points, closure rails, and frog are all the same polarity. Only the selected route is powered.

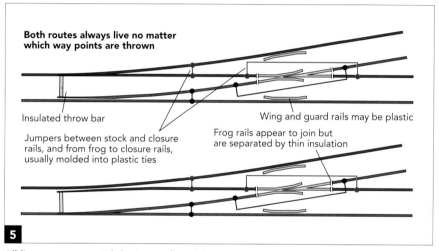

All-live turnouts avoid the issues found in many power-routing turnouts and lessen the chance of short circuits.

6. Characteristics of commonly available turnouts

Manufacturer	Type	Frog	Points	Modifications
Atlas	All live	Isolated metal	Insulated	Power the frog
Micro Engineering	All live	Isolated metal	Insulated	Power the frog
Peco Electrofrog	Hybrid	Metal	Insulated	Convert to all live per instructions and power the frog
Peco Insulfrog	All live	Plastic	Insulated	Add bonding jumpers
Shinohara (old)	Power routing	Metal	Connected	Convert to all live
Walthers Shinohara	All live	Metal	Insulated	Power the frog

shut off power by simply aligning the turnout back to the main line. The bad side is that having both frog rails the same polarity can result in a short if they are not electrically isolated from the diverging tracks. This is usually done by either installing plastic rail joiners or cutting gaps in the frog rails near the frog. Also because of this,

installing two power-routing turnouts back to back can create short circuits.

Another problem is that if a metal wheel derails while passing through a turnout it can simultaneously contact the point and closure rails of opposite polarity, leading to a dead short. Finally, if a locomotive's front wheels cross over the isolating gaps of the frog

rails it can create a short. This calls for extra attention on the part of engineers and can lead to interruptions with DCC due to booster shutdowns.

Another potential problem is that electrical continuity depends on the physical contact between the points and the adjacent stock rails. This electrical contact can be interrupted by ballast, corrosion, dirt, dust, paint, glue, or scenery materials.

All-live turnouts, **5**, avoid the issues found in many power routing turnouts by separating the points electrically, connecting points and the closure rails electrically to their adjacent stock rails, isolating the frog and powering it through a switch to control its polarity, and separating the frog rails and connecting them electrically to the stock rails of the proper polarity.

These features help avoid the kind of short circuits that can happen in power-routing turnouts, although it does mean you will have to do a little more wiring to power the frog. All-live turnouts are sometimes marketed as "DCC friendly" because they prevent these shorts.

Why are short circuits such an important issue with DCC? For example, a 5A booster operating at 14V puts out about 70 watts under a short circuit. This much power passing through a very small pathway—such as the spot where a locomotive wheel touches the track—can quickly become very hot. If the track has been wired correctly and the booster is working properly it will shut down and prevent any damage. However, under a worst-case scenario you can melt plastic parts, weld wheels to rails, and even start fires. Also, when the booster does shut down, operations (including all trains in that power district) come to a halt.

For these reasons I either use DCC-friendly turnouts on my layout or convert my old "unfriendly" turnouts to a better configuration—I'll show you how to do that later in this chapter.

You can also leave frogs unpowered. Peco Insulfrogs are one such type. These have a very short frog to help locomotives get over the unpowered section of track. Also, because most locomotives made today have all-wheel

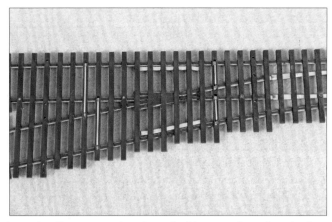

Many modern turnouts, such as this Walthers HO model, have their stock rails connected to the point/closure rails and to the frog rails using jumper wires or metal strips molded into the ties.

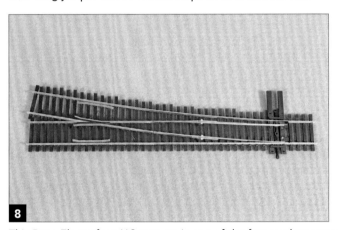
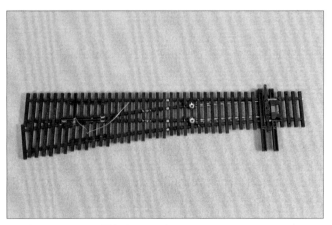

This Peco Electrofrog HO turnout is one of the few modern power-routing turnouts still being made.

electrical pickup, they don't tend to stall as on dead frogs as much as older models. However, with some other types of all-live turnouts the frog is a bit longer. Variations in the track can also cause wheels to lift as they go through a turnout, leading to stalling. For this reason I highly recommend powering your frogs.

The chart in **6** lists how several manufacturers deal with the issues we just discussed. I have also included information on an old Shinohara power-routing turnout for comparison and will show how to convert it to DCC-friendly configuration later in this chapter. All current turnouts I'm familiar with now provide isolated points and at least the ability to isolate the frog if it's not already isolated. Several also have the stock rails connected to the point/closure rails and to the frog rails using internal jumper wires or metal strips molded into the ties, **7**. On turnouts without this arrangement I would add jumper

wires to improve electrical continuity. In some cases the frog rails are powered by extending the electrical connection from the closure rails under the frog to the frog rails.

The only modern power-routing turnout in the table is the Peco Electrofrog, **8**. However, it can be converted to a DCC-friendly turnout by cutting a pair of jumper wires to isolate the frog and then routing power to the frog using the wire provided for this purpose. I also recommend adding jumper wires to the frog rails and closure rails and cutting through the rails on the diverging side of the frog to isolate the frog rails. Otherwise you have to install insulated rail joiners between the frog rails and diverging rails. This also helps prevent short circuits when a locomotive's wheels cross the gap at the frog rails. If the frog rails are isolated and connected to the live rails, then a locomotive can get almost to the frog itself without causing a short.

There are advantages to each type of turnout, and I know modelers who even mix them on the same layout. Personally, I think all-live turnouts are easier to wire and create fewer problems with respect to short circuits than power-routing turnouts, **9**. All-live turnouts are also the most common style available.

On the other hand, power-routing turnouts allow you to provide power to a single track based on how the turnouts are aligned, **10**. This is especially useful with conventional DC cab control when operating multiple engines within the same electrical block. The folks I know who use power-routing turnouts with DCC do so to take advantage of the power-routing feature. They install them on locomotive storage tracks and then kill power to them using the turnout. This helps extend the life of decoders, insures that they don't creep off, and also cuts down on the sound level in the room.

Wiring power-routing turnouts

For now let's assume that you are using DC cab control and power-routing turnouts on your new layout. How do you install them without creating a bunch of short circuits? There are just two simple rules for installing power-routing turnouts—any other tips and tricks are just an extension of them.

Rule 1 is to always attach power feeders off the point ends of turnouts. With power-routing turnouts, since the point rails are the same polarity, you will end up with a short circuit at one of them if power is fed from the frog end, **11**.

Rule 2 is to gap the rails between any turnouts when placed frog-to-frog, **12**. Again, this prevents feeding power to a turnout through the frog end. Even in very complex layout designs these two rules will keep you out of trouble.

Quick fixes

There are situations where you might want to modify your turnouts to make them more reliable and prevent shorts. Figure **13** shows a simple way to avoid the problem of poor electrical contact between points and stock rails on power-routing turnouts. By using auxiliary contacts on a switch machine and soldering feeder wires to your stock rails and frog, you will always

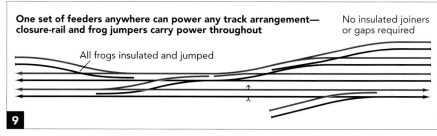

One set of feeders anywhere can power any track arrangement— closure-rail and frog jumpers carry power throughout

All frogs insulated and jumped

No insulated joiners or gaps required

9

All-live turnouts are easier to wire and create fewer problems with respect to short circuits than power-routing turnouts.

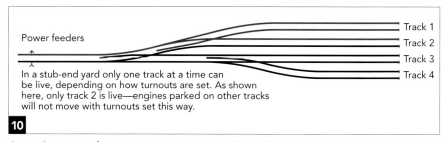

Power feeders

Track 1
Track 2
Track 3
Track 4

In a stub-end yard only one track at a time can be live, depending on how turnouts are set. As shown here, only track 2 is live—engines parked on other tracks will not move with turnouts set this way.

10

One advantage of power-routing turnouts is they allow you to provide power to a single track based on how the turnouts are aligned.

have reliable power.

Similarly, by cutting gaps in the closure rails and adding jumper wires between the stock and closure rails you can insure that the polarity of the point rails will always match the adjacent stock rails, **14**. This modification prevents short circuits should a metal wheel bridge the gap between them. That drawing also shows how these modifications can be used with all live turnouts if they don't already have them.

Upgrading turnouts

Let's tackle the more-complex job of making an old power-routing turnout DCC friendly. The basic idea is to reduce the potential for short circuits. Keep in mind that you can usually convert a DC-powered layout to DCC without going back and modifying all of your track and turnouts. However, addressing these issues may make your life easier in the long run, especially if you are building a new layout. You may also find that some of these

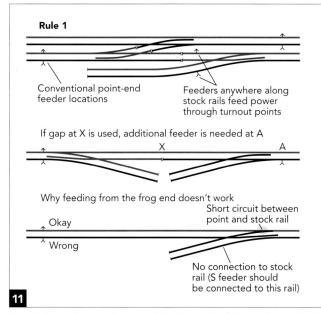

Rule 1

Conventional point-end feeder locations

Feeders anywhere along stock rails feed power through turnout points

If gap at X is used, additional feeder is needed at A

X   A

Why feeding from the frog end doesn't work

Short circuit between point and stock rail

Okay

Wrong

No connection to stock rail (S feeder should be connected to this rail)

11

Rule 1 is to always place track feeders off of the point ends of turnouts.

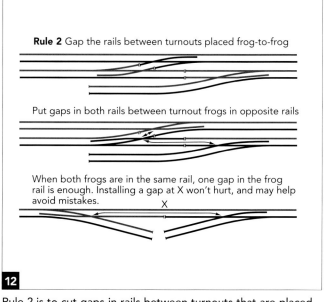

Rule 2 Gap the rails between turnouts placed frog-to-frog

Put gaps in both rails between turnout frogs in opposite rails

When both frogs are in the same rail, one gap in the frog rail is enough. Installing a gap at X won't hurt, and may help avoid mistakes.

X

12

Rule 2 is to cut gaps in rails between turnouts that are placed frog to frog.

modifications (especially adding jumpers) can be used with some all-live turnouts as well.

The drawing in **15** shows what features a DCC-friendly turnout should have. To convert turnouts, I isolate the frogs, power the frogs using a mechanism to switch polarity, reinstall the points so they are powered independently, and tie the closure rails and points electrically to the stock rails using jumpers. Let me take you step by step through the process.

Step 1: Isolate the frogs by cutting through the rails on each side using a motor tool and cutting disk, **16**. To keep the rails apart, glue a small styrene shim in each opening and then trim it to match the rails, **17**. After painting, the shims are barely noticeable.

Step 2: If you're using Caboose Industries or other ground throws without auxiliary contacts to switch polarity, wire the isolated frog using a feeder wire soldered to the side of the frog away from the aisle, **18**. Connect the feeder wire to a Frog Juicer, **19**, to control polarity (more on those in Chapter 8).

If you use a Tortoise or other switch machine with auxiliary contacts, then these can be used to control the polarity of the frog.

Step 3: The points on old Shinohara turnouts are electrically connected through solder joints to metal strips at the throw bar and where they meet the closure rails. This means the open point is always the opposite polarity of its adjacent stock rail. Even though there's a gap, if the back of a metal wheel bumps the point (or a derailment occurs), it will create a short and shut down the booster. This can also lead to damage if the booster is slow to shut down (or if the circuit breaker fails).

The closure rails are electrically connected to the frog so they are the same polarity as well. Electrical connections are made where the point rails contact the stock rails and through a metal strip under the points and closure rails. All of these connections depend on a tight physical contact that often works loose or is interrupted by dirt or grime.

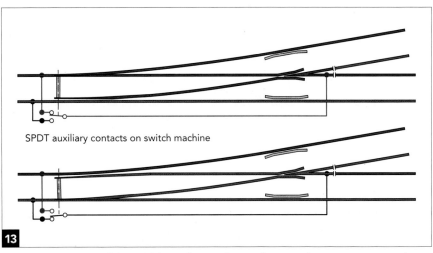

SPDT auxiliary contacts on switch machine

13

Here's a way to avoid the problem of poor electrical contact between points and stock rails on power routing turnouts.

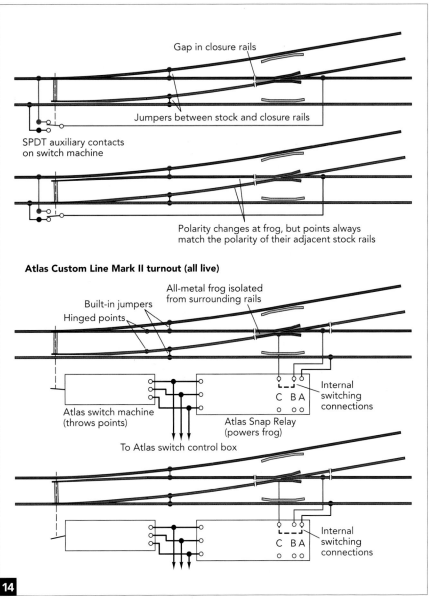

Gap in closure rails

Jumpers between stock and closure rails

SPDT auxiliary contacts on switch machine

Polarity changes at frog, but points always match the polarity of their adjacent stock rails

Atlas Custom Line Mark II turnout (all live)

All-metal frog isolated from surrounding rails

Built-in jumpers

Hinged points

Atlas switch machine (throws points)

Atlas Snap Relay (powers frog)

C B A

Internal switching connections

To Atlas switch control box

C B A

Internal switching connections

14

Isolating frogs and adding jumper wires can go a long way toward making turnouts of all types more trouble-free.

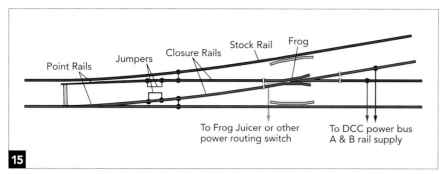

Point Rails
Jumpers
Closure Rails
Stock Rail
Frog

To Frog Juicer or other power routing switch

To DCC power bus A & B rail supply

15

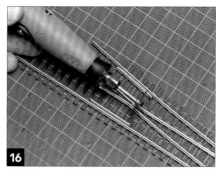

16

DCC-friendly turnouts have isolated frogs that can be wired independently, points the same polarity as adjacent stock rails, a direct electrical connection between stock and closure rails, and a direct electrical connection between the closure rails and points.

A motor tool with a cutting disk makes isolating frogs quick work.

17

Install styrene shims in the gaps on each side of the frog, left, then trim the shims to match the rail profile, right.

18

19

By soldering feeder wires to the sides of the frogs facing the backdrop, they will be out of sight after installation.

A Frog Juicer (made by Tam Valley Depot) works well for controlling frog polarity where a switch machine with auxiliary switching contacts is not used. These can be attached to the underside of the layout with double-sided foam tape.

To fix this, drill out the rivets holding the point rails in place, **20**. Measure the distance between them at the point ends. Using a soldering iron, disconnect the points from the metal strips that hold them together, **21**. Use needlenose pliers to pull the metal strips from under the ends of the closure rails and a sharp no. 11 knife blade to cut off the plastic support.

Slide rail joiners onto the ends of the closure rails, **22**. It may help to slip a no. 17 knife blade under the ends of the closure rails to make room for the rail joiners to slide into place. Then slip the points into the open end of each rail joiner. The fit should be tight enough to firmly hold the points in gauge and still allow their ends to move about ⅛" to each side. A pair of needlenose pliers is useful for

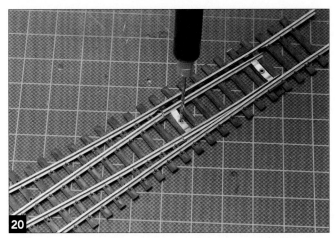

20 Drill out the rivets that hold the points to the plastic ties.

21 Use a soldering iron to separate the points from the metal strips that hold them together.

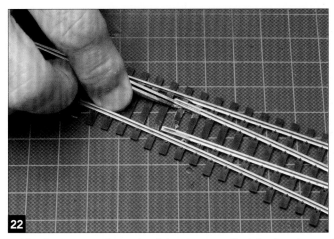

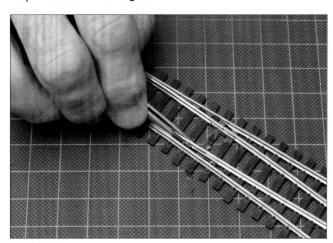

22 Add rail joiners to the ends of the closure rails, left, then insert the points into the rail joiners, right.

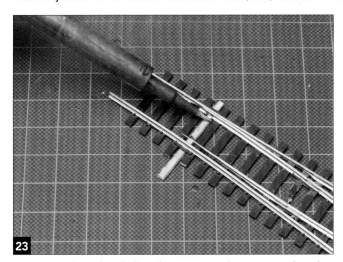

23 Insert a PC-board tie below the points as the new switch rod, then solder each point in place.

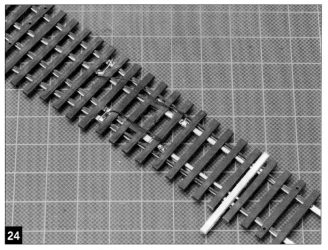

24 Jumper wires installed between the stock and closure rails and the closure rails and points provide a reliable electrical connection.

tightening the rail joiners.

Cut a new throw bar from Clover House copper-clad PC-board tie strips and slide the new throw bar into the opening underneath the points. Solder each point to the copper tie using the measurements made from the old points, **23** (see Chapter 11 for tips on soldering). File a notch through the copper surface in the middle of the throw bar to electrically isolate the two points.

Step 4: At this time, the points and closure rails are connected and electrically independent, but still

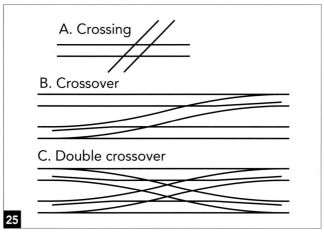

A. Crossing

B. Crossover

C. Double crossover

25

Crossings allow routes to cross at grade. Crossovers allow trains to move between parallel tracks.

26

All track manufacturers offer crossings in a several angles and rail sizes. No special wiring is needed for these.

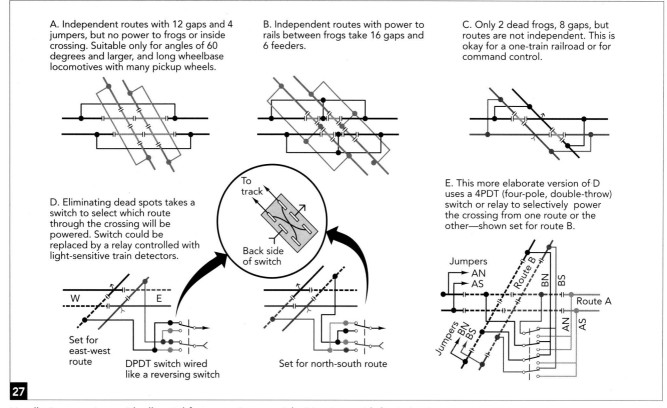

A. Independent routes with 12 gaps and 4 jumpers, but no power to frogs or inside crossing. Suitable only for angles of 60 degrees and larger, and long wheelbase locomotives with many pickup wheels.

B. Independent routes with power to rails between frogs take 16 gaps and 6 feeders.

C. Only 2 dead frogs, 8 gaps, but routes are not independent. This is okay for a one-train railroad or for command control.

D. Eliminating dead spots takes a switch to select which route through the crossing will be powered. Switch could be replaced by a relay controlled with light-sensitive train detectors.

To track

Back side of switch

E. This more elaborate version of D uses a 4PDT (four-pole, double-throw) switch or relay to selectively power the crossing from one route or the other—shown set for route B.

W   E

Set for east-west route

DPDT switch wired like a reversing switch

Set for north-south route

Jumpers
AN
AS

Route B

BN   BS

Route A

Jumpers
BN
BS

AN

AS

27

Handlaying crossings with all-metal frogs requires special wiring to avoid short circuits.

depend on physical contact with the stock rails for power. Fix this by soldering short jumper wires between the stock rails and closure rails on each side of the turnout, and then run a short jumper wire between each closure rail and the point attached to it, **24**. This guarantees that the point and closure rails will always be the same polarity as their respective stock rails, lessening the chance of shorts, and will never have to depend on physical contacts for power in the turnout.

Crossings, crossovers, and slip switches

Crossings, **25**, allow two tracks to cross one another at grade without changing routes. Several companies make crossings with plastic insulated frogs, **26**, in a variety of angles. These have jumpers imbedded in the plastic frogs to guarantee electrical continuity, and the plastic frogs are usually short enough that most locomotives can reliably run through them. If you handlay crossings with metal frogs you'll need to do some

special wiring, **27**. Because of this complexity I highly recommend purchasing commercial crossings.

A crossover allows trains to move from one parallel track to another, **25**. The easiest way to make a simple crossover is to place two turnouts across from each other, oriented frog to frog, and follow two-rail wiring rules (**11, 12**). A double crossover, **25**, is a bit more complex, allowing trains to cross from parallel tracks going in either direction. They are useful at entrances

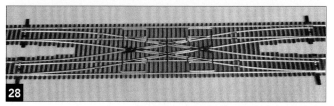

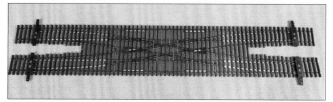

Double crossovers, like this one from Walthers, have all the required wiring connections already imbedded in the plastic.

A. Wiring double crossover with ready-to-use crossing

Gaps in outer rails at X and Y are optional, but if used require an additional N feeder at A and an S feeder at B

B. How it works

Internal gaps and jumpers of ready-to-use crossing not shown

As set for for one crossover route. Wiring works just as well if both crossover routes are set, though both routes can't be used simultaneously.

C. Wiring double crossover with all-rail frogs in crossing

All crossing frogs isolated. Center frogs have their own permanent N and S feeders

Outer frogs powered through jumpers from SPDT auxiliary contacts on switch machines (contacts N have no connections)

With one crossover route set, outer frogs are correctly powered through auxiliary contacts. Turnout controls must be arranged so that only one crossover route at a time can be set to avoid short circuits through outer frogs.

29

Should you decide to handlay a double crossover or purchase an old one without internal jumpers, follow these wiring suggestions.

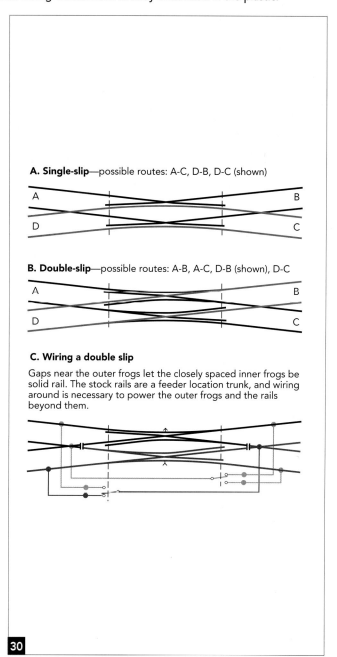

A. Single-slip—possible routes: A-C, D-B, D-C (shown)

B. Double-slip—possible routes: A-B, A-C, D-B (shown), D-C

C. Wiring a double slip

Gaps near the outer frogs let the closely spaced inner frogs be solid rail. The stock rails are a feeder location trunk, and wiring around is necessary to power the outer frogs and the rails beyond them.

30

Slip switches are a combination of a crossing and a turnout with multiple routes through them. They are typically used in yards where speeds are slow and space is tight.

to staging yards, large passenger stations, and other busy areas. As with crossings, double crossovers are available with all the required connections already imbedded in the plastic, **28**. Should you decide to hand-build one, follow the wiring guidelines in **29**.

Slip switches, found in yards and other tight switching areas, are a combination of a crossing and a turnout with multiple routes through them, **30**. Commercially available versions marked as DCC-friendly have internal jumpers to simplify wiring.

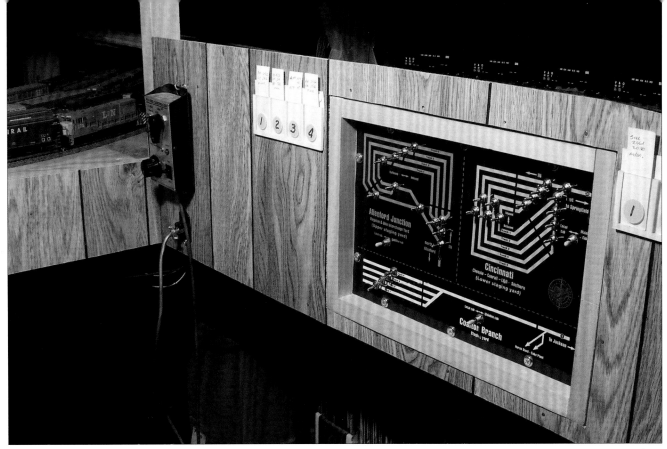

Jim Hediger

CHAPTER FIVE

Cab control for DC

Jim Hediger still uses conventional DC cab control with additional local throttles on his large HO scale Ohio Southern layout. The toggle switches on the control panel at right control block power for two staging yards and a branch line. One of the layout's walkaround-style plug-in throttles is hanging at left.

With standard DC power, as long as you only want to operate one train on your layout at a time, then you only need wiring for one power pack. However, as soon as you decide to run two or more trains, things get a bit more complicated.

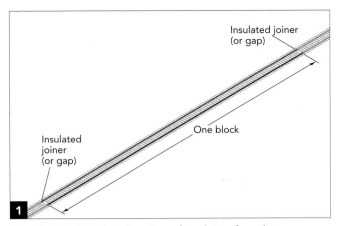

1 Any electrically isolated section of track is referred to as a block. Gaps in one or both rails isolate the block.

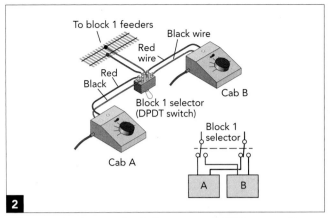

2 Cab control in its most basic form uses a DPDT center-off switch to select the cab controlling a block.

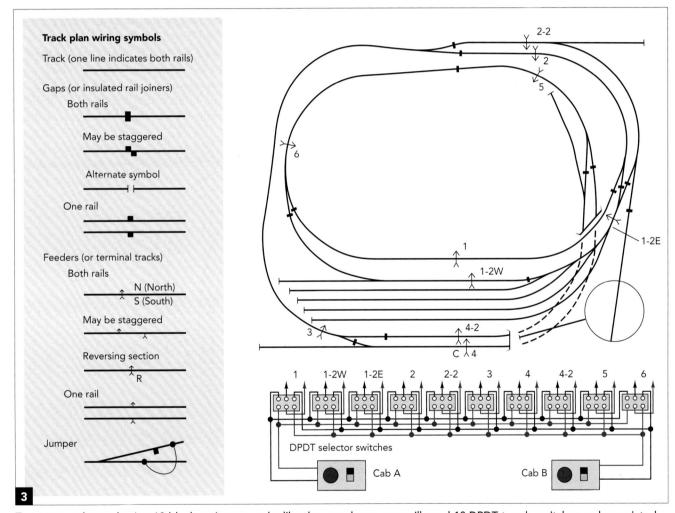

Track plan wiring symbols

Track (one line indicates both rails)

Gaps (or insulated rail joiners)
Both rails

May be staggered

Alternate symbol

One rail

Feeders (or terminal tracks)
Both rails
N (North)
S (South)

May be staggered

Reversing section
R

One rail

Jumper

3 To operate a layout having 10 blocks using two cabs like the one shown, you will need 10 DPDT toggle switches and associated wiring to select the cab controlling each block.

Cab control has been the most common form of multiple-train-control wiring for standard DC operation since the early days of the hobby. For those who choose not to use Digital Command Control (DCC), it remains a viable alternative.

Blocks

Cab control involves wiring your layout into a series of electrically isolated sections of track called *blocks*, **1**. Only one independently controlled train can be within any single block at one time. Cab control with two power packs is called *dual cab control*.

Each block requires wires to connect it to either of two power packs, and a toggle or slide switch to select which power pack controls the block. Electrically isolated blocks are created by cutting through the rails at the

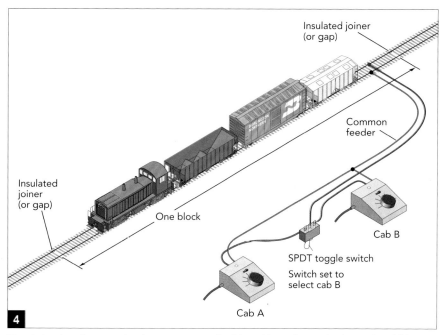

Here's basic cab control using common-rail wiring. Note that only the red and blue control wires are connected to the SPDT switch, which is used to route power from one cab to the track.

beginning and end of the desired block (or using insulated rail joiners) and providing separate power connections to each block. As your train moves around the layout you have to set the turnouts for your desired route, switch on power to the next block ahead of your train, and then switch off power in the block you just left.

Block length can be difficult to determine. If you make blocks too long, you limit the flexibility in having multiple trains in one area. But if you make them too short, it can become a real juggling act to throw all those block switches while at the same time controlling your locomotive's speed. And if someone forgets to do one of these steps, or connects a power pack to the wrong block, the next thing you know you will be asking "who's controlling my train?" A rule of thumb is that blocks should be at least as long

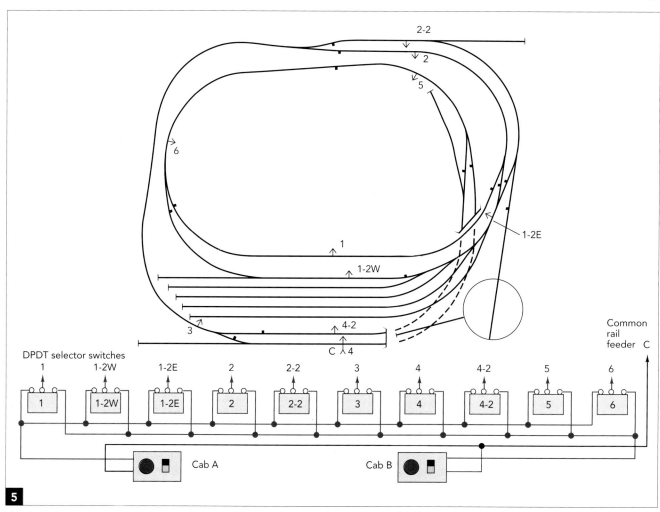

This is the same layout as shown in **3** but with common-rail wiring—both layouts have all-live turnouts. Notice the reduction in the number and complexity of wires.

as the longest train you plan to operate, plus a little extra.

In addition to your mainline blocks, you can also create local blocks with their own power packs to isolate operations in yards and industrial switching areas. This allows yard switchers and local freights to do their jobs while the mainline trains roll by. These dedicated blocks can be further subdivided; for example, to allow two switchers to work opposite ends of a yard.

If you have an engine terminal in a yard, you probably will want to have a dedicated inbound and outbound track so your hostler can move locomotives in and out of the roundhouse or off a service track. All of this is done with more toggle switches that allow you to route power from specific power packs to the desired sections of track.

Cab control

How do you go about setting up blocks for operating two mainline trains? Here's where cab control comes in. The basic principle is easy to understand. Each power pack or throttle on a model railroad is considered a cab. In its simplest form, all you need to control two trains is a double-pole, double-throw (DPDT) switch—usually a toggle switch with a center-off position—to route power from one of the two cabs to the block you want to control, **2**. The two variable DC wires from each cab are attached to the outside contacts on the DPDT switch. A pair of wires from the middle two contacts are run to the block to be powered. By simply flipping the DPDT switch to the left or right, you

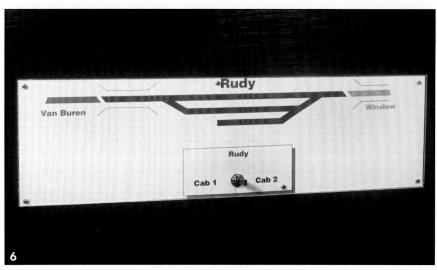

This local panel on a fascia has the track diagram with a toggle switch for control.

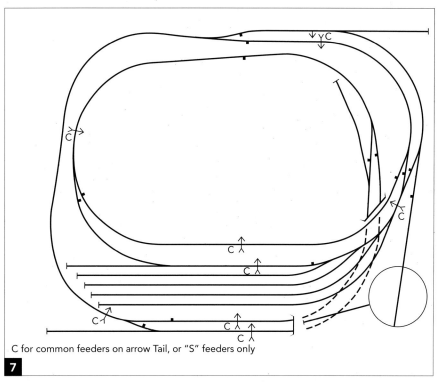

C for common feeders on arrow Tail, or "S" feeders only

Common-rail wiring does require a few more connections between the common bus and the common rail when using power routing turnouts.

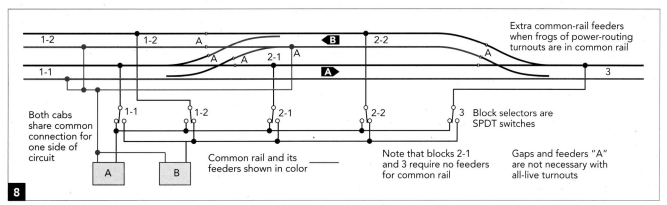

Because of their power-routing feature, power-routing turnouts require additional gaps, even on the common rail.

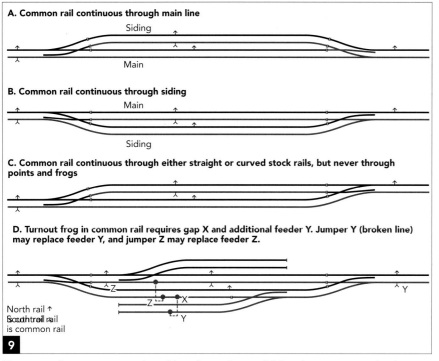

A. Common rail continuous through main line

Siding

Main

B. Common rail continuous through siding

Main

Siding

C. Common rail continuous through either straight or curved stock rails, but never through points and frogs

D. Turnout frog in common rail requires gap X and additional feeder Y. Jumper Y (broken line) may replace feeder Y, and jumper Z may replace feeder Z.

North rail ↑
South rail
is common rail

9

Here are a few more examples of locations where additional gaps are required to isolate power-routing turnouts.

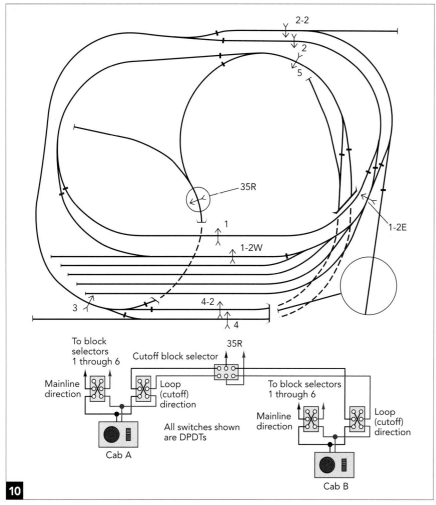

10

Turning tracks require an additional reversing switch in order to correct track polarity.

can control which cab is powering the selected block. If you have 10 blocks on your layout then you will need 10 DPDT switches, one for each block, **3**.

The most important thing when wiring these switches is to be consistent with your connections so that the wires from the same cab are connected to the same rails when the route is selected. Many published track plans include wiring symbols like those shown in **3**, making it a lot easier to keep your wiring consistent and trouble free.

Organizing all these toggle switches so that your engineers know which switch controls which block is an important part of cab control. Small layouts often have one central control panel with the block selector switches installed at midpoints within each block on a schematic drawing of the tracks. On larger layouts you may need to divide your control panel into smaller sub-panels located around the layout. You'll see examples throughout the book; I'll provide more details on designing and building control panels in Chapter 9.

Common-rail wiring

One way to simplify the wiring for cab control is to use common-rail wiring. With common-rail wiring, one rail is used as a common return for both cabs, **4**. Note that the black wire is connected to both cabs and to one rail. The red and blue wires from a single-pole, double-throw (SPDT) switch are connected to Cab A and Cab B respectively. Finally, the red control wire to the track is connected to the SPDT switch that selects which cab controls the block. The simplification comes from the fact that only one wire is run from each toggle switch to the track, eliminating almost half the number of individual wires used in **3**.

The other connection to the track is a single common wire connected directly to each cab, **5**. Another simplification can be seen in **4**, as only one of the two rails has gaps cut in it. With common-rail wiring, one rail is continuous, with the exceptions we'll see below. Whichever wiring method you use, the toggle switches look the same on the panel side, **6**.

As discussed in Chapter 4, there are a number of situations where using power-routing turnouts requires additional gaps to prevent short circuits. This need to cut additional gaps means that there will be places where the common rail itself must be gapped, and that's where you lose the common-rail connection. To guarantee electrical continuity with the rest of the common rail, additional feeders from a common bus will be required at any location where the common rail is gapped, **7**.

For example, where frogs of power-routing turnouts are in the common rail, you will need a gap and additional feeders, **8**. There are a few other situations where gaps and feeders are required with various configurations of sidings, **9**. Even though you end up adding more gaps and feeders with power-routing turnouts, the common-rail method will still reduce the overall complexity of your wiring.

There is one additional limitation with common-rail wiring—you cannot power multiple throttles using the same power supply. This isn't a problem when using multiple power packs. However, if you power a homemade throttle using the accessory DC power provided by a commercial power pack which is also being used on the layout, that would create a short circuit.

Wiring reversing loops

In Chapter 7 we'll take a much more in-depth look at ways to turn locomotives and even whole trains. For now, let's take a quick look at the wiring involved in adding a reverse loop with cab control. As an example we'll add a reversing loop to the layout diagram we've been working with in this chapter. The configuration shown in **10** assumes basic two-rail wiring and all-live turnouts. The main additions required for the reversing loop are the reversing switches for both the main line and the reversing loop itself. These are required whether you use common-rail wiring or not, **11**.

As you can see, common-rail wiring still cuts down on the number of feeders that are required between the

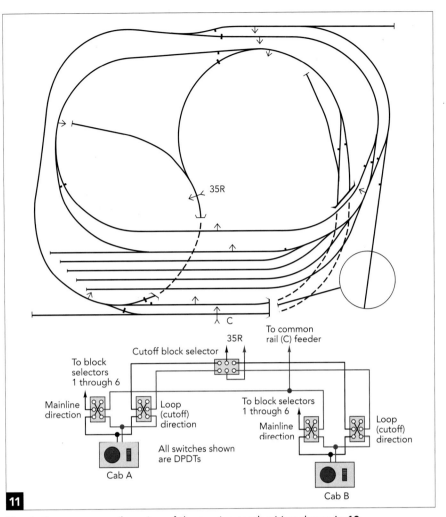

11 Here's the common-rail version of the turning track wiring shown in **10**.

12 Centralized control panels can be made to look like dispatcher's panels. This is Jim Hediger's HO Ohio Southern, which uses four-position rotary switches for control.

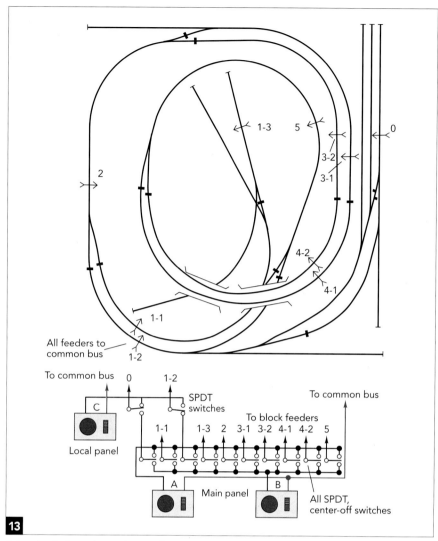

A local-priority cab can be used to operate a switcher in a yard or a town.

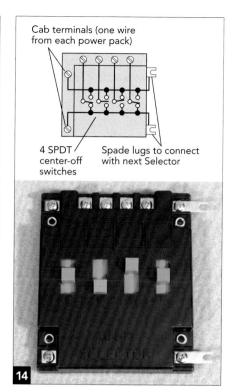

The Atlas Selector contains four DPDT slide switches. It's designed specifically to be used for selecting cabs.

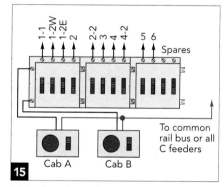

Multiple Atlas Selectors can be connected for cab control.

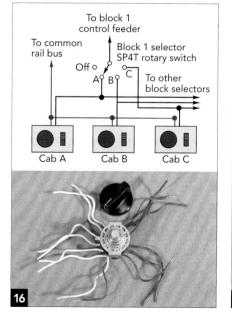

Operating more than two trains requires switches with multiple positions like this rotary switch.

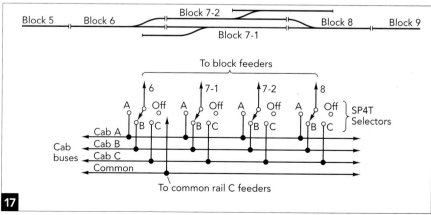

Walkaround operations can be implemented using rotary switches placed at various locations around the layout.

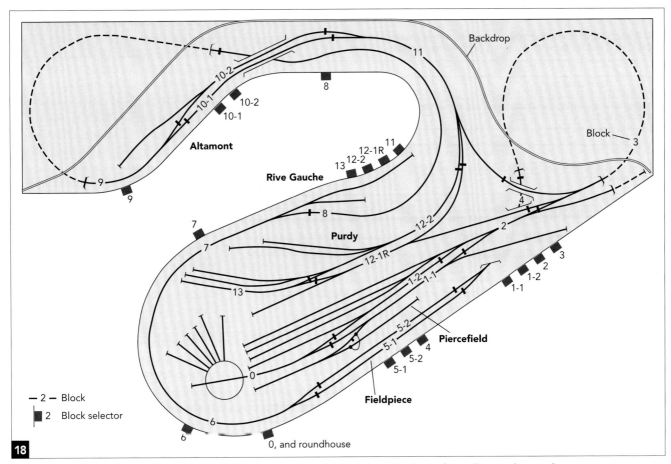

18

Here's an example of a mid-size layout with block cab selectors located on the fascia for walkaround control.

Here's an example of three Atlas Selectors being used in a central location.

track and the common bus. Should you decide to use power routing turnouts with this layout you would need to add the gaps and feeders as in **7**.

Adding a local cab

Panels can be centralized either at the layout or, as in **12**, at a dispatcher's panel, where a dispatcher selects the blocks. Earlier in this chapter I mentioned the value of adding local cabs to layouts. Having these additional

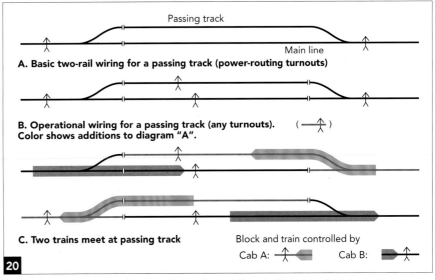

Passing sidings require that parallel tracks be electrically isolated. This can be achieved by using block gaps at one end along with power-routing turnouts, or gapping both ends with any kind of turnouts. This arrangement allows one train to be isolated on the passing siding while the other continues on the main line.

cabs allows switchers to operate in yards or towns and industries without interfering with mainline trains. This can greatly increase the operating potential of a layout, so let's take a

look at how it's done. In **13**, you can see a small yard located on the right side, designated as block 0. There is also a passing siding off the main line, identified as block 1-2, which also

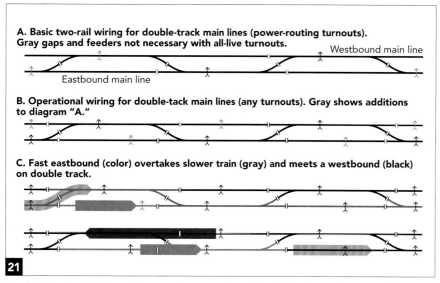

A. Basic two-rail wiring for double-track main lines (power-routing turnouts). Gray gaps and feeders not necessary with all-live turnouts.

Westbound main line

Eastbound main line

B. Operational wiring for double-tack main lines (any turnouts). Gray shows additions to diagram "A."

C. Fast eastbound (color) overtakes slower train (gray) and meets a westbound (black) on double track.

21

Double-track main lines allow greater operational flexibility for trains to pass but require more block gaps in order to do it.

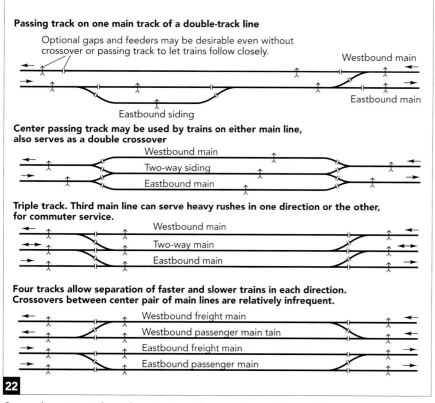

Passing track on one main track of a double-track line

Optional gaps and feeders may be desirable even without crossover or passing track to let trains follow closely.

Westbound main

Eastbound siding

Eastbound main

Center passing track may be used by trains on either main line, also serves as a double crossover

Westbound main
Two-way siding
Eastbound main

Triple track. Third main line can serve heavy rushes in one direction or the other, for commuter service.

Westbound main
Two-way main
Eastbound main

Four tracks allow separation of faster and slower trains in each direction. Crossovers between center pair of main lines are relatively infrequent.

Westbound freight main
Westbound passenger main tain
Eastbound freight main
Eastbound passenger main

22

On medium-size to large layouts, two, three, and even four track arrangements can ease train movements.

serves as the entrance to the yard.

As the diagram shows, cab C has been added as the local cab, with two SPDT switches between the cab and the block feeder. These two switches allow the two mainline cabs (A and B) to operate locomotives in block 0 and 1-2 as well as the local cab. This arrangement allows the switcher to

interact with the mainline trains to add or remove cars, or for the yard tracks to be used for staging trains.

By using power-routing switches in the yard, you could park a locomotive (or a locomotive consist) while its train is being made up, then you can isolate the switcher while the train pulls out of the yard.

Atlas Selectors and Controllers

Atlas has for many years made the Selector switch, **14**, designed specifically for use with dual-cab control. The Selector is basically four SPDT switches with a center-off position in each. Because they incorporate SPDT switches, they are designed specifically to be used with common-rail wiring. Each Selector has spade lugs and screw terminals at opposite ends, allowing them to be daisy-chained in series, **13, 19**.

Another Atlas device, the Controller, is designed for reversing loops. It looks similar to the Selector but contains two mainline direction switches, a reversing loop block selector, and reversing loop direction switch. Controllers also have spade lugs and screw terminals allowing them to be daisy chained to control one or multiple reversing loops and to connect with one or more Selectors. The Atlas website (atlasrr.com) has more information on these components, as well as publications specific to using them. A downside is that their design doesn't lend them to be used on schematic-design control panels, which is why experienced modelers tend to prefer conventional toggle switches.

Adding more cabs

Now that you know how to simultaneously operate two mainline trains using DC cab control, let's consider the complexity involved in wiring a layout to operate four, five, or six trains all at once.

The most common way to do this is using multi-position rotary switches, **12, 16**. For every block on your layout you will need a selection switch with all the wiring associated with it to connect the throttle to the block you want to control, **17**. These can be installed on local panels scattered around the layout or mounted in the fascia in front of the blocks they control, **18**. To select which cab is controlling a specific block, all you do is rotate the switch to that cab and the rest is the same as with dual-cab selector switches.

The complexity of the wiring increases (as does the expense) of this method as the number of blocks and

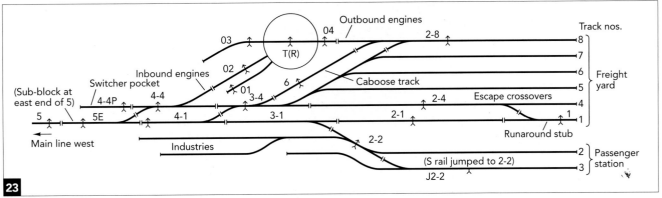

23

Complex yards require multiple blocks to allow switchers and road locomotives to be operated simultaneously.

size of the layout increases. For larger layouts, you'll probably find it more cost-effective to consider making the switch to Digital Command Control if you want to control more than two trains at once.

Locating blocks

Now that you know how to wire your layout for cab control, let's consider where you need to place your blocks. If you are modeling a single-track main line, then you obviously need places where trains can meet or pass—these are called passing sidings, **20**. When two trains are scheduled to meet at a passing siding, one must take the siding while the other passes it on the main line. In order to do this, the sidings must be electrically isolated as separate blocks. This requires the rails to be gapped, and for better operations additional gaps are desirable. Each long section of single track between sidings can be wired as one long block or subdivided to allow trains to follow one another closely.

On double-track main lines additional blocks increase operating flexibility, allowing fast trains to pass slower ones on the same track, **21**. Three- and four-track main lines, **22**, add even more flexibility but are rare on model railroads due to the space required. The four-track arrangement in **23** is similar to the track arrangement once used by the Southern Railway in its Washington Division yard at Monroe, Va. This arrangement was used for separating passenger and freight trains where a busy main line passed through the middle of the yard.

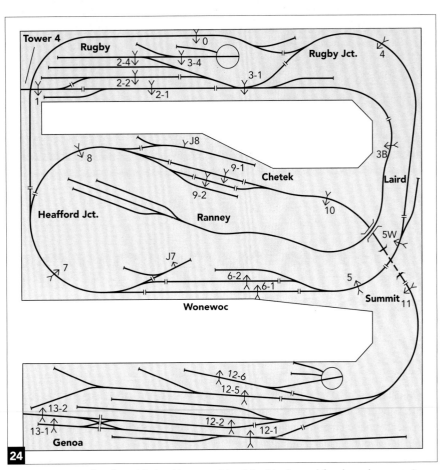

24

Here's an example of a mid-sized layout with all its blocks and feeders shown, using power-routing turnouts.

Large yard complexes can require numerous blocks for prototypical operations, **23**. The block and feeder arrangement shown allows yard switchers to make up trains while road engines are serviced and moved in and out of the yard, all while passenger trains come and go at the passenger station.

Block and feeder arrangements for a mid-sized layout designed for a lot of road switching operations, **24**, can actually appear simpler than the yard in **23**. Notice how the branch line up to Ranney is operated as one large block, since only one train would be on that stretch of track at one time. The longer sections of mainline track between the yards at Rugby and Genoa give plenty of room for trains to operate while keeping the blocks to reasonable lengths.

Model Railroader collection

CHAPTER SIX

Wiring a layout for DCC

Wiring a layout for Digital Command Control involves installing components such as command stations and boosters under the layout. Visible panels, such as the EasyDCC panel at right, can include local throttles.

As we saw in Chapter 5, it can be a complicated undertaking to wire even a mid-sized model railroad to operate more than two trains at the same time using conventional DC power. Model railroaders have always wanted a reliable way to run multiple trains without all the hassles of block wiring, so when Digital Command Control (DCC) came along, modelers went for it in a big way. In this chapter, we'll look at the big picture for wiring DCC layouts, and get into the finer details in following chapters.

In the early days of DCC, some modelers were reluctant to make the switch. The biggest roadblock wasn't wiring—it was decoders. Few locomotives were available with factory-installed decoders, and adding a decoder usually meant hard-wiring all the connections. That has changed in the past decade or so. Most mid-level to high-end model locomotives are now available with DCC (and even sound) decoders installed, and many after-market decoders are designed for specific models, making installation much easier.

Recent surveys from *Model Railroader* magazine show that about 40 percent of modelers now use DCC, with numbers continuing to climb. In my local area, I couldn't find any layouts of significant size still using multi-cab DC controls—everybody has switched to DCC, and that's what I'm going to recommend to you. So let's dig into the details of operating more than two trains on a layout using DCC.

DCC wiring

The main differences in wiring a DCC layout compared to DC is that the wires are heavier, there are more feeders, and there are far fewer blocks. Plus, there are no cab control switches to deal with. Most properly wired DC layouts can be converted to DC simply by connecting your booster in place of one power pack and switching all block controls to that cab. The only reason you need blocks for DCC is to divide the layout into more manageable subsections for power distribution, block detection, and signaling.

As we saw in Chapter 5, common-rail wiring can greatly simplify DC cab-control wiring. However, there are no such advantages (and even some disadvantages) to doing the same with DCC. One reason for this, as we will see in later chapters, is that you can't rely on the rails as a common conductor with DCC the way you can with DC. With DCC, long bus runs can create problems including having a single common-rail bus. With DCC your boosters and command station have to be optoisolated for use with common rail wiring.

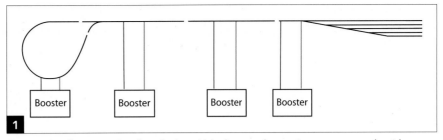

One option for powering four isolated blocks on a layout is to power each with a separate booster.

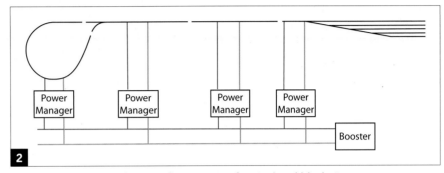

Another more-practical option for powering four isolated blocks is to use one booster and four power management circuits.

The bottom line is to avoid common-rail wiring for DCC. If you're converting from a common-rail DC layout, I suggest you add the few extra feeders and rail gaps to convert it. It will make your DCC wiring simpler and easier to debug in the long run.

Blocks for DCC

The great thing about DCC is that you can control as many locomotives as your booster can power with just two wires going to the track. For many small layouts, you may be able to get by using just one large power block. However, for most medium-size to large layouts, breaking the layout up into a few blocks or *power districts* can make operations a lot smoother and more reliable.

The question many ask is if you can operate as many trains as your booster can power in one block, why bother with creating more? The primary reasons for having blocks on a DCC layout are to isolate short circuits to a smaller area (and isolate short-prone areas), balance power needs to limit putting all of a layout's power on the track at once, and install a signal system.

The one weakness of DCC is its sensitivity to short circuits. Few things are more frustrating when running

trains than having all trains suddenly shut down and wait while a short is cleared because someone ran through a closed turnout or derailed while switching. Short circuits like these are inevitable, but by breaking up a layout into smaller operating segments you can prevent a short in any one area from stopping operations in all the others. Yards and industrial switching areas with their numerous turnouts are prime areas for short circuits. By placing them in their own blocks you can isolate potential problems.

A small layout may only require a few amps to operate all trains, while the power needs on larger layouts can easily exceed what a 3- or even 5-amp booster can provide. By dividing the layout into several blocks, each with its own power source, you can balance your power needs and increase your layout's operating capability.

Block occupancy detectors and signals can be installed by dividing the layout into blocks. Multiple detection and signal blocks can be located within a single power block, but each detection block must still must be electrically isolated from all others. I'll get into installing detection and signal systems in Chapter 12.

Wiring a large layout as a single

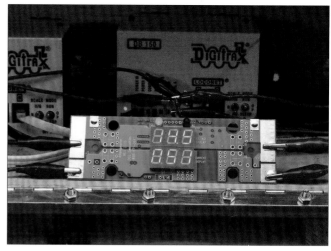

The DCC Specialties RRampmeter is capable of measuring the voltage and amperage of a DCC power bus. It can be used as a portable meter or wired into the bus feed from the booster to check voltage and amperage.

large block would require a large booster, which can cause some undesirable consequences. So as soon as we start creating power blocks, we have to have a way to power each one. One option is to provide a separate booster for each block, **1**, but that can get expensive, and it's overkill. There's another option in the middle that will work well for most layouts.

Power management

Power management allows you to take the power from one booster and divide it among several electrically isolated blocks, **2**. Power management devices work by assigning a certain amount of current from the booster to each block with the total actually exceeding that of the booster—but how does that work? The concept is based on the assumption that it is unlikely that the maximum amperage will be required in all blocks at the same time. It's similar to your house wiring: The overall service at your breaker box is 100 amps, but if you add all the individual 10-, 15-, and 20-amp circuits with their own breakers, the total is well over 100. This works because you don't have all of your lights, appliances, and other gadgets on at the same time.

Relating this to a layout, trains spend a lot of time sitting and use little if any power when they do. Let's assume you have four blocks on your layout and when trains are running in them you need about 2.5 amps for each block for a total of 10 amps. Without

power management you'd either have to buy a couple of 5A boosters, one 10A booster, or a combination of smaller boosters. With power management you may be able to use a single 5A booster to cover the 10A total.

How is this any different from just using one booster to power all the blocks? First, power management devices provide a circuit breaker for each block. This isolates short circuits and also prevents the amperage from exceeding an assigned trip current value. The circuit breaker in each power manager circuit will prevent an overload in any one block from shutting down the booster and stopping operations in other blocks.

Why not use a simple 5A circuit breaker in each block? One limitation to power management is the total amperage actually being used in all the power-managed blocks at any one time cannot exceed the rated capacity of the booster powering them. So if you underestimate your power needs or just end up running more trains than you expected, you can exceed the booster's maximum rating and it will shut down. As your power needs change over time due to changes in your operating scheme or layout expansion, you may need to either adjust the block power assignments or add another booster. So you do have to spend a little time balancing the power management scheme.

Developing a balanced power management scheme requires that you estimate the typical current demand

within each block. When doing this, keep in mind the age of your locomotives and whether they have sound or extra lighting. For example, my old HO Atlas S2 diesel switchers run at about .6 amps each; however, my new Broadway Limited 4-8-4 steam locomotive maxes out at just .3 amps, even with sound and lights on.

Another consideration is whether your passenger trains are lighted or you have accessory decoders drawing power from the track bus. Anything that takes power from your track bus must be added in. (One of the best ways to measure your power needs would be to wire a DCC Specialties RRampmeter, **3**, into the block bus and measure the average and maximum current draw directly.)

Finally, enter the trip-current value into the power manager, and then be prepared to make adjustments in power assignments once you've operated the layout a few times. The other option is to make an educated guess and update your settings once you operate the layout a few times.

Power managers

There are a couple of options for power management: cheap/low-tech or more-expensive/high-tech.

The low-tech approach, called a *ballast lamp*, has actually been around for decades. It uses 12-volt automobile bulbs, **4**, in the block circuit. The idea is to place one of these bulbs in line with the block you want to protect.

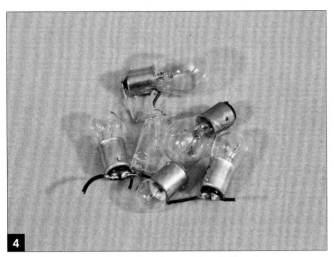

Automotive taillight bulbs can be used as ballast lamps to reduce the impact of short circuits.

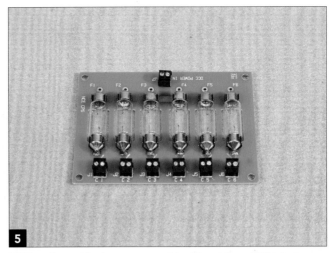

NCE makes a block protector with either 1A or 1.75A bulbs as ballast lamps.

The Digitrax PM42 power manager is a relay-based device.

The PSX-4 power manager features all solid-state electronics.

Here's how it works: Under normal operating conditions, the bulb filament simply conducts the operating current of the trains. However, if a short circuit occurs, the full amperage of the booster flows through the bulb and lights it, limiting the track current to that of the bulb. The bulb will stay on until the short is cleared.

The most commonly used bulb is a no. 1156 auto bulb rated at about 2.5A, but there are other low-amperage alternatives. For example, NCE makes a block protector with either 1A or 1.75A bulbs, **5**.

There are pros and cons for using ballast lamps. On the pro side, they are cheap and the light gives an unmistakable indication of where the problem is. On the con side, fast-acting boosters may actually trip before the bulb lights (the bulb is not as fast-acting as the high-tech methods), multiple shorts may shut down the booster, and the bulb can stay on and get hot, potentially damaging nearby plastic parts if it's not noticed. Personally, I feel the cons outweigh the pros, so I don't use ballast lamps to protect entire blocks.

Now for the high-tech approach. Several manufacturers offer power management devices and they use two different switching technologies: *relay* and *solid state*. For examples I'm using the Digitrax PM42 (relays) and the DCC Specialties PSX-4 (solid state).

Although the Digitrax PM42, **6**, is designed for that company's systems, it potentially can be used with any DCC system. The main limitation is that programming must be done with a Digitrax throttle or a computer program that can emulate such a throttle.

Programming is required to change the trip current value for the blocks (the default is 3A), and to change the speed at which the circuit trips (there are four options,) as well as various other functions. It can be configured for protecting four blocks as either a circuit breaker or automatic polarity reverser or a combination of the two (although this reduces the total number of blocks that can be managed).

Maximum amperage for the blocks can be set from 1.5A to 12A in .5A increments. Although wiring the four outputs can appear difficult, especially for combinations of overload and polarity, I found it fairly straightforward once I actually did it, but it does require good soldering skills. The circuit board is powered by a separate 14-16V transformer. Should you find that you need more power

8 Some manufacturers install small fans in their boosters to cool them. This is MRC's Prodigy Advance.

9 Digitrax installs a large heat sink on the rear of the booster enclosure itself.

10 The easiest way to deal with excess heat is to install a small fan to blow directly on the booster.

than is provided by a single booster, you can add another and rebalance the four outputs. The main limitation of the PM42 is that the same trip current value applies to all four blocks—you can't have one block set to 3A and the rest set to 1.5A each.

DCC Specialties produces the Power Shield series of power managers typically referred to as PSX, **7**. The trip current can be set from 1.27A to 17.8A in 1.27A increments and can be programmed using either jumpers that you solder onto the board or DCC ops mode programming. Unlike the PM42, because the PSX circuits are electrically independent, you can set different trip current values for each block. There are numerous other features including system feedback, detection, and onboard and remote status lights, and they don't require a separate power supply. The devices can be programmed by all the major DCC systems and can interact with their control buses. In addition, instead of having selectable trip speeds, they use an intelligent logic algorithm that can discern the difference between a short circuit and the current load caused by the in-rush current of sound decoders powering up.

One convenient feature of the PSX is that it is available in several configurations. This is an important consideration when deciding whether you want your power managers all in one place or distributed around the layout near the blocks they power. The Digitrax PM42 has all four power manager circuits on a single board, so all your wiring has to

fan out from one location.

The PSX power managers are available with one, two, three, and four circuits on a single board, so you can scatter various combinations of them around the layout with their boosters and reduce the lengths of your wiring runs. Also, because the circuits are completely independent, if you purchase a board with multiple circuits they can later be separated along the provided score lines if you decide to go from a central to a distributed configuration as described in Chapter 3.

Be aware that low-output boosters can create problems, since they may not be powerful enough to stay on if the power manager has to cycle on and off repeatedly during a full short circuit. To counter this problem, the PSX can be configured to remain off in case of a such a short, and then can be restarted using a remote switch. The unit also offers a power-boost mode which helps some boosters start even with heavy sound decoder loads—a problem I ran into with my old Athearn Genesis Challenger.

Preventing overheating

Most boosters share a common weakness in that they generate heat internally. This heat is a byproduct of the electrical components used in the circuits and the need to decrease the input voltage to the level needed on the tracks. Under normal operating conditions, most boosters can run all day without heat being an issue. However, if boosters are placed next to a heat source, in a confined or sunny

location, or run for long periods near their maximum operating amperage, excess heat will build up inside the enclosure. For this reason some manufacturers install small fans in their boosters to cool them, **8**. Others attach their power transistors to the inside of the enclosure and use it as a heat sink, or install a large heat sink on the enclosure itself, **9**.

But even boosters with large heat sinks may not be able to get rid of the excess heat. To prevent damage to sensitive components, boosters have temperature sensors that automatically shut the booster down when the internal temperature exceeds a critical value. Consequently, most 5A boosters can only maintain a sustained output of about 3A.

With power management, we may operate our boosters closer to the maximum sustained amperage more of the time so we may need a way to deal with the excess heat. The easiest way to deal with this issue is to place a small external fan so it blows directly on the booster, **10**. If you have all your boosters in one location you can build a box for them and install a small computer fan in it to keep them cool, **11**.

Locating blocks

Now that we know what power managers and blocks do, let's take a look at a couple of examples of how to divide blocks starting with a typical small layout. When choosing blocks I usually start by isolating yards and switching areas with lots of turnouts. Next I go for staging yards, and finally

11

If you have all your boosters in one location, you can build a box for them and install a small computer fan in it to keep them cool.

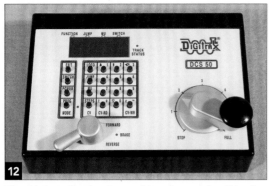

12

The Digitrax Zephyr is capable of supplying 3A of power.

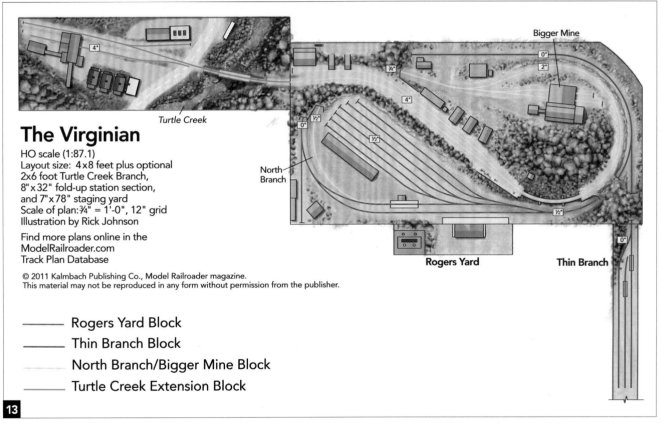

Bigger Mine

Turtle Creek

North Branch

The Virginian

HO scale (1:87.1)
Layout size: 4×8 feet plus optional
2×6 foot Turtle Creek Branch,
8"×32" fold-up station section,
and 7"×78" staging yard
Scale of plan: ¾" = 1'-0", 12" grid
Illustration by Rick Johnson

Find more plans online in the
ModelRailroader.com
Track Plan Database

© 2011 Kalmbach Publishing Co., Model Railroader magazine.
This material may not be reproduced in any form without permission from the publisher.

—————— Rogers Yard Block

—————— Thin Branch Block

—————— North Branch/Bigger Mine Block

—————— Turtle Creek Extension Block

Rogers Yard

Thin Branch

13

The Virginian is a small HO layout that can be operated using a fairly low-powered DCC system. The main advantages to be gained from dividing it into blocks is in isolating areas prone to short circuits.

I block out long runs of single- or double-track main line. Let's look at small and large examples.

Model Railroader's 50-square-foot HO scale Virginian project layout, which appeared in the January through June 2012 issues, was wired as one large block. The staff used a 1.5A NCE PowerCab DCC system capable of simultaneously operating two to three HO locomotives. Because of the low-amperage output of this system, it's hard to get much advantage from power management other than

isolating Robers Yard and the Thin Branch staging yard.

To avoid this issue you could use a slightly more-powerful 3A system such as a Digitrax Zephyr, **12**. The layout, **13**, could be divided into four blocks: 1) Rogers Yard shown in red, 2) the North Branch and Bigger Mine shown in yellow, 3) the Thin Branch shown in blue, and 4) the Turtle Creek extension shown in green. Using a PM42, you could assign a 1.5A trip current to all four blocks for a total of 6A powered by the 3A booster. This would prevent

the short circuits in each block from shutting down operations on the whole layout.

Power management really shines on medium-size to large layouts like Eric Brooman's original Utah Belt layout, **14**. You could break this 325-square-foot layout into at least five blocks: 1) the main yard at Benton shown in red, 2) Descanso and the long section of mainline trackage associated with it shown in yellow, 3) the long stretch of track from Tunnel no. 2 to Iron Mountain shown in blue, 4) the hidden

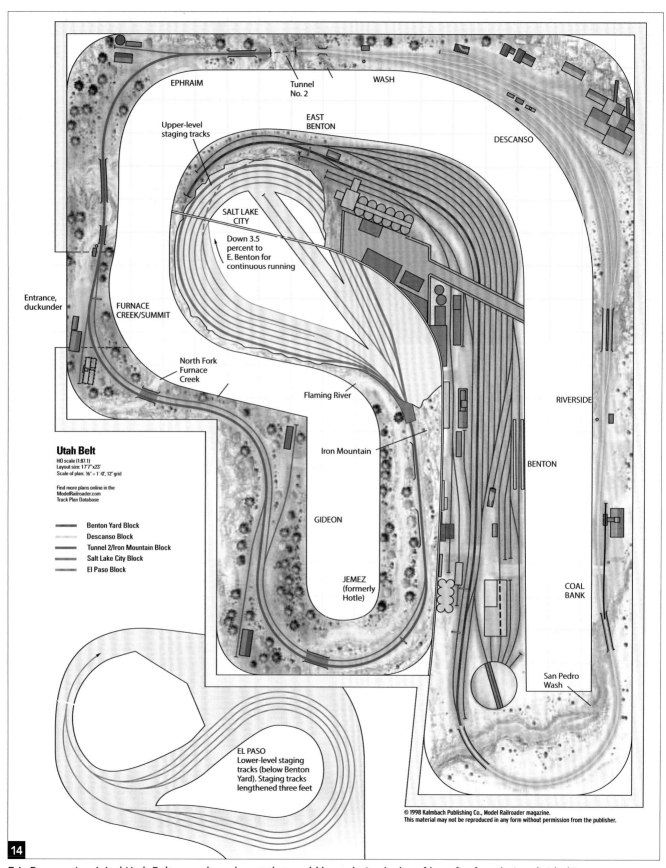

EPHRAIM

Tunnel No. 2

WASH

Upper-level staging tracks

EAST BENTON

DESCANSO

SALT LAKE CITY

Down 3.5 percent to E. Benton for continuous running

Entrance, duckunder

FURNACE CREEK/SUMMIT

North Fork Furnace Creek

Flaming River

RIVERSIDE

Iron Mountain

BENTON

Utah Belt
HO scale (1:87.1)
Layout size: 17'7"x23'
Scale of plan: ¾" = 1'-0", 12" grid

Find more plans online in the
ModelRailroader.com
Track Plan Database

GIDEON

COAL BANK

Benton Yard Block
Descanso Block
Tunnel 2/Iron Mountain Block
Salt Lake City Block
El Paso Block

JEMEZ (formerly Hotle)

San Pedro Wash

EL PASO
Lower-level staging tracks (below Benton Yard). Staging tracks lengthened three feet

14

Eric Brooman's original Utah Belt was a large layout that could have derived a lot of benefits from being divided into power management blocks. The large yard at Benton offers a lot of opportunities for shorts at turnouts and the reverse loops in Salt Lake City and El Paso create their own short circuit hazards, all of which can be isolated using power managers. Finally, power management should allow it to be operated with a single 8A booster.

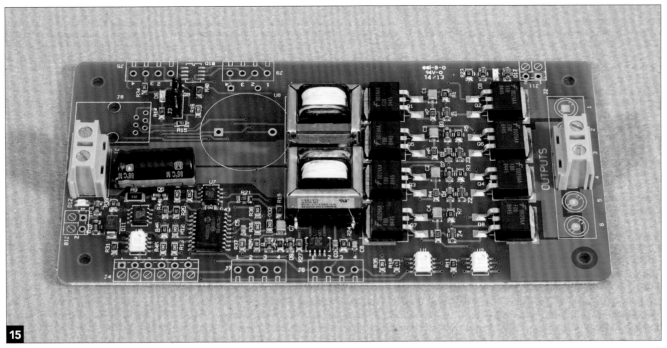

15

DCC Specialties' PSX-AR acts both as a power manager and auto reverser.

reverse loop and staging tracks in Salt Lake City shown in green, and 5) the hidden reverse loop and staging tracks in El Paso shown in orange. Using a PSX-3 I would start with a current draw of 3.81A for the Benton block and 2.54A each for the Descanso and Tunnel no. 2 blocks.

The two reversing loops require special attention. DCC Specialties also makes the PSX-AR, **15**, which adds auto-reversing to the PSX circuit board. You could use two of these set to 1.27A each to control the reverse loops and staging tracks at Salt Lake City and El Paso. Since the total potential current demand for all five blocks is 11.43A, an 8A booster could be used to power all the blocks. By placing the 8A booster and PSX units under the lower end of Benton yard, you should be able to keep power buses down to about 30 feet in length and avoid the issues I discuss below.

Staying in phase
In dealing with both DC and DCC wiring we often talk about maintaining the correct polarity. However, to be technically correct, with DCC we should be talking about maintaining the correct phase. The power on the two rails is out of phase and if the two come into direct contact it

has the same effect as a DC short. Consequently, when you hook up the two wires from the booster or power managers to the track, you always have to make sure that all the wires to a given track originate from the same output connection on the boosters. If you hook up a couple boosters or power managers to the track and your locomotives short out at the gaps between two blocks, the first thing to suspect is out-of-phase power feeds. Fixing this problem is as easy as reversing the two power feeds to the tracks.

Long power buses
Most home layouts are small enough that the length of the power bus isn't a concern. However, when operating multiple trains on large home layouts, clubs, and modular layouts, we can run into problems with power buses longer than 30 feet in length. Manufacturers have different ways of dealing with this issue, so it is best to check with system manuals and tech support staff if you plan long runs just to see what they recommend. If you don't experience any problems, regardless of how long your power buses are, then you don't need to do anything.

What are the potential issues with long power buses? Most folks are

familiar with the effects of resistance on DC power, but with AC power (of which DCC is a type), another electrical property is involved: *inductance*. Inductance can transform various types of electromagnetic noise—such as the constant making and breaking of contact at the wheel/rail interface—into transient voltage spikes that can have detrimental effects on the DCC signal. The magnitude of these effects is dependent on the length of the wires and the amperage on the bus.

The symptoms of problems associated with long bus runs include the loss of command signals resulting in loss of control, runaway trains, slow speeds, and voltage spikes large enough to cause a decoder to lose its programming or to even damage it.

How can we deal with these problems? The easiest way is to locate your boosters and other components so that all your buses are under 30 feet. One trick is to use a distributed booster network—instead of placing all your boosters in one common location, you can distribute them around the layout in or near the blocks they power, **16**. You can also place the booster in the middle of the block with the power bus extending out in each direction, turning a 60-foot run into two 30-foot runs, **17**.

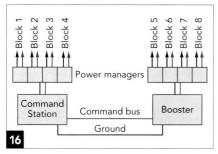

16

By placing power managers or boosters around your layout you can avoid long bus runs.

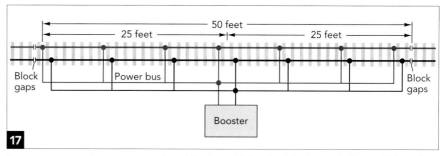

17

Boosters or power managers placed in the middle of a block also help avoid long bus runs.

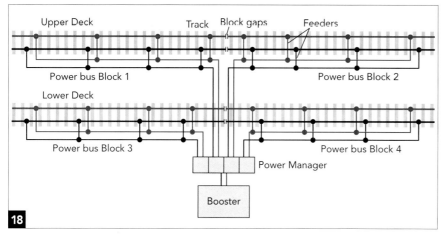

18

On my layout I have two power managers powering two blocks on the upper deck and two others that power two middle-deck blocks.

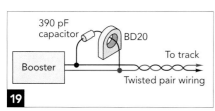

19

One trick developed by John M. Smith for detectors like the BD20 that use current sensing transformers is wiring a capacitor between the bus wires with one leg through the current-sensing transformer. It is important to wire the capacitor through the detector exactly as shown.

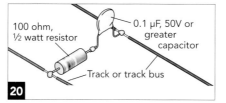

20

By adding a snubber of a resistor and capacitor between your power bus wires you can eliminate power spikes and the various problems that come with them. *Original diagram courtesy of North Coast Engineering.*

This gets a little complicated when using power managers. You have to add in all the wire it takes to go from the booster to the power manager, so they need to be kept as close together as possible. Thus you should distribute both your boosters and your power managers.

For example, on my triple-deck layout I have one centrally located 8A booster powering four PSX power managers. Two power managers power

two blocks on the upper deck and the other two power two middle-deck blocks, **18**. The wires from each are then attached to 30-foot-long buses powering 60-foot-long blocks on each deck. I have an additional 5A booster located in another remote location that powers two staging yards and a couple of additional blocks using a similar power manager arrangement.

Another way to deal with these issues is to use twisted-pair wiring and snubbers. By simply adding about three twists per foot to your power buses

you can eliminate many problems. The twisting should be done before the wires are installed. Be aware that this might make adding feeders problematic. Twisting wires can result in false detects with block occupancy detectors, but this can be easily dealt with by placing your detectors as close to the detected section of track as possible and then not twisting the wires after the detector.

Another trick when using detectors that use current sensing transformers, developed by John M. Smith, is wiring a capacitor between the bus wires with one leg through the current-sensing transformer, **19**. Also, avoid bundling wires of different buses together— separate them by a few inches. The same is true for command and throttle networks—always keep them about six inches from the power buses.

Decoder-killing power spikes require a different approach. By adding a snubber made up of a resistor and capacitor between your power bus wires or rails you can eliminate power spikes and the various problems that come with them, **20**. These should always be placed at the end of the bus. In cases where you have two buses supplied by a centrally located booster or power manager, a snubber should be placed at the end of each bus.

Only use snubbers if you have power buses longer than 30 feet, you measure large voltage spikes on your tracks, or are experiencing problems with decoders losing their programming or being destroyed. Some manufacturers (including Digitrax) do not recommend them, so check with your manufacturer's tech support staff before using them.

CHAPTER SEVEN

Reverse loops and wyes

Any time a piece of track turns back on itself, allowing a locomotive or complete train to be turned, it creates the potential for a short circuit. Reverse loops, wyes, and turntables are all used on model railroads to turn locomotives and trains. Handling these areas is critical regardless of the type of control system you're using. Fortunately there are a number of easy ways to deal with them. We'll start with reverse loops on standard DC layouts, then look at how they can be handled with DCC.

On Jim Vail's HO Glenwood & Black Creek, the helix that connects the two decks also provides reverse loops in both directions. Reverse loops require special wiring whether a layout is wired for DC or DCC.

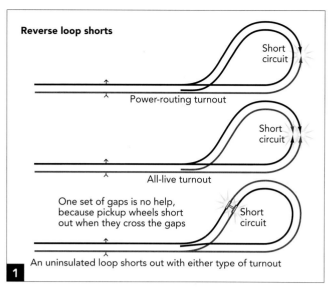

Reverse loop shorts

Short circuit

Power-routing turnout

Short circuit

All-live turnout

One set of gaps is no help, because pickup wheels short out when they cross the gaps

Short circuit

An uninsulated loop shorts out with either type of turnout

1

When the rails forming a reverse loop turn back on themselves, it creates a short circuit at the point where they are of opposite polarity.

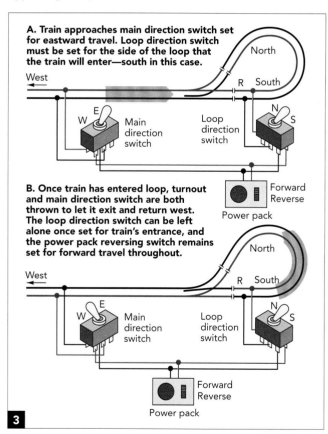

A. Train approaches main direction switch set for eastward travel. Loop direction switch must be set for the side of the loop that the train will enter—south in this case.

North

West

R South

E
W Main direction switch

Loop direction switch

N
S

Forward Reverse

Power pack

B. Once train has entered loop, turnout and main direction are both thrown to let it exit and return west. The loop direction switch can be left alone once set for train's entrance, and the power pack reversing switch remains set for forward travel throughout.

North

West

R South

E
W Main direction switch

Loop direction switch

N
S

Forward Reverse

Power pack

3

By throwing the switch so the polarity is correct when the train enters the loop, then changing the mainline polarity, the train does not have to be stopped.

A. One-switch method

Mainline feeders

Two pairs of gaps

Reversing-section feeders

R

DPDT switch wired as a reversing switch, loop direction switch

Power pack

To feeders

From power pack

B. Two-switch method

Main line direction switch

Loop direction switch

R

Power pack

2

A DPDT reverse switch is typically used for controlling reverse-loop polarity. One approach (top) is to wire the switch in the feeders between the power pack and the reverse loop. This approach requires the train to be stopped when the reversing switch is thrown. A more-realistic option (bottom) is to use two reversing switches, one for the mainline feeders and the other for the reverse-loop feeders.

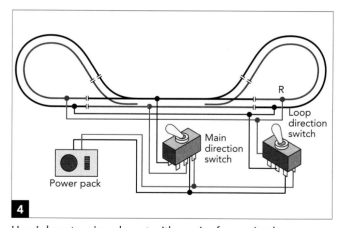

R

Main direction switch

Loop direction switch

Power pack

4

Here's how to wire a layout with a pair of reversing loops separated by a section of mainline track.

Reverse loops

The reverse loop is the most common method for turning trains on a model railroad. The drawing in **1** shows that when the rails forming a loop turn back on themselves it creates a short circuit because they are of opposite polarity. The simplest way to prevent this is to electrically isolate the section of track forming the loop to create a reversing block. This is done just like you create any other block by simply cutting through both rails at each end of the desired block.

The reverse loop block needs to be as long as your longest train, since the metal wheels of your locomotives and cars will create a short as they cross the

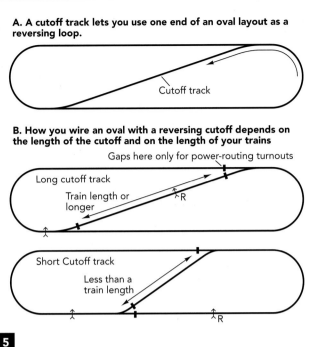

A. A cutoff track lets you use one end of an oval layout as a reversing loop.

Cutoff track

B. How you wire an oval with a reversing cutoff depends on the length of the cutoff and on the length of your trains

Gaps here only for power-routing turnouts

Long cutoff track

Train length or longer

R

Short Cutoff track

Less than a train length

R

5

A. The dogbone layout gives the appearance of a double track where tracks are parallel and allows continuous running. However there is no way to turn a train.

B. By adding switches and crossovers at the "X's", you can add operational flexibility while allowing trains to revers direction. It also creates reversing sections, shown in red, that must be dealt with.

X   X

6

A cutoff is a section of track that cuts across an oval or large loop, forming a reversing loop. This is straightforward on a small layout, but cutoffs can sometimes be hidden on large layouts.

The venerable dogbone layout contains loops at each end but the tracks don't actually connect back on themselves so a short isn't created (top). However, adding a crossover between the tracks (bottom) creates a reverse loop.

gaps—it's not enough to only have the block as long as your longest locomotive consist. Once the train is isolated in the reverse loop, you need to have a way to correct the polarity before it can exit the loop. There are two ways to do this with a double-pole, double-throw (DPDT) toggle switch, **2**.

The simplest method is to wire a single DPDT reversing switch between the power pack and the feeders powering the reversing section of the loop. To run a train with this arrangement, start by setting the DPDT switch so that the reverse loop's polarity matches the section of main line from which it will enter the loop. Run the train into the reverse loop and then stop it before the locomotive crosses the gaps at the other end of the block. Throw the reverse switch on your power pack. This reverses the polarity of the mainline rails. You must also throw the DPDT reversing switch for your reverse loop. With the polarity of the reverse loop rails now matching the mainline rails, align the turnout, start your train in motion, and continue on your way.

Obviously all this starting and

stopping leaves a lot to be desired as far as realistic operation is concerned. A more realistic option is to use two DPDT reversing switches, one for the mainline feeders and the other for the reverse loop feeders, **2**. In running a train with this wiring configuration, start by setting the loop DPDT switch so the loop polarity matches the main line, **3**. Run the train into the reverse loop and, when it's completely in the loop, throw the mainline DPDT switch to change the polarity of the mainline block. Finally, align the turnout so the train can exit the loop. With this method the train does not have to be stopped while polarity is corrected. The diagram in **4** shows how to wire your layout for this approach if you have a pair of reverse loops separated by a section of mainline track on your layout.

Cutoff tracks are another type of reverse loop commonly used in many small layouts. A cutoff is basically a section of track that cuts across an oval or large loop, forming a reversing loop at one end, **5**. They are easily handled using the methods in **2** and **3**.

There are also similar configurations

that at first glance—especially on larger layouts—may not seem to be a reversing loop. For example, the venerable basic dogbone layout, **6**, contains loops at each end but the tracks don't actually connect back on themselves. However, some similar plans add a crossover between the tracks at one end, creating a reverse loop. These can also be wired using one of the methods just described.

Flipping all these toggles takes away from the realism we try to achieve when operating our layouts, but there's a way to partially automate the process. You can use the auxiliary contacts on a switch machine to do most of the work for you, although each method has a drawback, **7**. Using the first configuration shown, once the train enters the reverse loop you throw the switch for the turnout and the auxiliary contacts reverse the polarity of the main line. This method means the train does not have to be stopped in the reverse loop, but it does create a problem if another train is operating elsewhere in a mainline block. The second approach shown in **7** does require stopping the train in the reverse

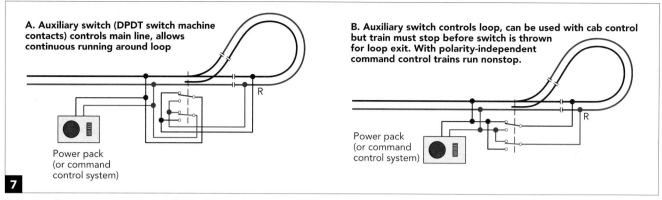

B. Auxiliary switch controls loop, can be used with cab control but train must stop before switch is thrown for loop exit. With polarity-independent command control trains run nonstop.

Power pack (or command control system)

Power pack (or command control system)

7

Using auxiliary contacts on a switch machine makes it possible to partially automate reversing loops. With the train in the reverse loop, throw the switch for the turnout and the auxiliary contacts reverse the polarity of the main line. This approach requires stopping the train in the reverse loop before throwing the switch for the turnout but it doesn't change the polarity of the main line.

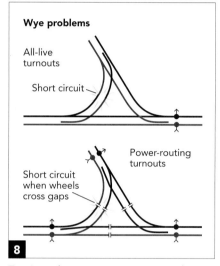

Wye problems

All-live turnouts

Short circuit

Power-routing turnouts

Short circuit when wheels cross gaps

8

Turning a locomotive in a wye involves running the locomotive from the through track onto one leg of the wye and backing it onto the tail track. Align the turnout for the other leg, then proceed forward onto the through track. A short is created whether you use power-routing or all-live turnouts.

loop before throwing the turnout, but it does not change the polarity of the main line.

Wyes

Wyes are triangular track arrangements that allow a locomotive—or in some case a whole train—to be turned. A wye can be a junction between a main line and a branch line which allows trains to go on different routes, or a stub-ended track off a main line or yard track designed specifically for turning trains.

Turning a locomotive on a wye involves running the locomotive from the through track onto one leg of the wye, **8**. The locomotive is backed along the leg to the tail track, where the turnout is then aligned for the other leg of the wye. At that point the locomotive is advanced down the other leg of the wye and through the turnout onto the through track.

As you can see in **8**, a short is created whether using power-routing or all-live turnouts. It is easy to correct this problem using either a reversing switch or the auxiliary contacts on a switch machine, **9**. That drawing shows how to wire the wye if you have enough room to reverse a whole train, using one leg of the wye as a reversing section instead of the tail track.

Turntables

With turntables, you need to insure that the polarity of the turntable track is correct before running a locomotive onto it. You also need a means to reverse the polarity of the rails when the turntable turns 180 degrees.

Three options for correcting rail polarity are shown in **10**. The first method uses a simple DPDT toggle switch to reverse polarity. The key is remembering to flip the switch anytime the table is rotated more than 180 degrees.

A more-commonly used method uses a split ring rail in the turntable pit to automatically reverse polarity. As the pickup wheels on the turntable bogies pass over the gap in the ring rail the polarity of the turntable rails is reversed. The throttle must be turned off all the way while the table

is turning (usually not an issue on a turntable), otherwise there will be a short circuit as the bogie wheels cross the gaps.

A third method employs a common stereo phone plug and jack available from electronics suppliers. The plug is built into the turntable with the two wires for the rails attached to it. The jack is installed below the turntable pit, allowing the turntable to be plugged into it. The contacts on the jack are then wired to a reversing switch (just like the first method), which is manually thrown to correct polarity when the turntable is rotated.

Polarity indicators

With the above types of reversing tracks it's necessary to make sure that track polarity is correct before a train enters a reversing section. Exactly how can we do that?

It's easy to install a couple of light bulbs that will indicate when it's safe to proceed. The configuration in **11** shows how to use a red or green bulb to indicate whether it is safe to enter or leave a reverse loop. The drawing also shows how to wire both a green and red bulb across any rail gaps to indicate when polarity is correct or not. These bulbs can be installed as trackside signals on the layout itself or on a control panel.

Depending on your track voltage and the voltage rating of the bulbs, you may need to install a small dropping resistor in line with the bulb. You can also substitute light-emitting diodes (LEDs) for bulbs by wiring a 670- to

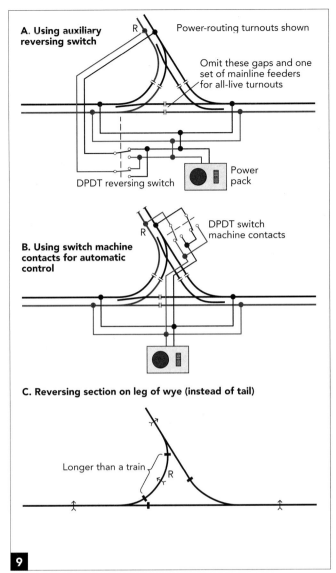

A. Using auxiliary reversing switch

Power-routing turnouts shown

Omit these gaps and one set of mainline feeders for all-live turnouts

DPDT reversing switch

Power pack

B. Using switch machine contacts for automatic control

DPDT switch machine contacts

C. Reversing section on leg of wye (instead of tail)

Longer than a train

9

You can easily correct the short in the wye using either a reversing switch or the auxiliary contacts on a switch machine. If you have enough room to reverse a whole train, using one leg of the wye as a reversing section instead of the tail track you can use this approach.

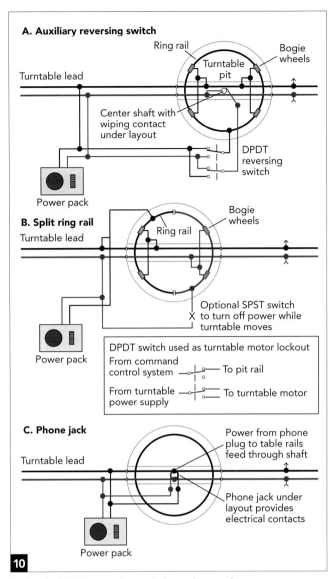

A. Auxiliary reversing switch

Ring rail

Bogie wheels

Turntable lead

Turntable pit

Center shaft with wiping contact under layout

DPDT reversing switch

Power pack

B. Split ring rail

Bogie wheels

Turntable lead

Ring rail

Optional SPST switch to turn off power while turntable moves

Power pack

DPDT switch used as turntable motor lockout

From command control system → To pit rail

From turntable power supply → To turntable motor

C. Phone jack

Power from phone plug to table rails feed through shaft

Turntable lead

Phone jack under layout provides electrical contacts

Power pack

10

A simple DPDT reversing switch can be used to reverse turntable polarity. You can also use a split ring rail in the turntable pit to automatically reverse polarity. Another option is to use a stereo phone plug with the contacts on the jack wired through a reversing switch (like in **10a**) to correct polarity when the turntable is rotated.

1000-ohm resistor between the track and the LED.

Autoreversing for DCC

The good news is that everything discussed so far also works with DCC, except in most cases it can be simpler and easier! The reason DCC simplifies the process for correcting short circuits is that locomotive direction is controlled internally by the decoder and is independent of track polarity. This means you can throw a DPDT reversing switch while a train is running through a reverse loop and the locomotive will keep running in the same direction at the same speed, although there may be a momentary hesitation as the contacts switch.

This means that by simply wiring the switch machine auxiliary contacts as a reversing switch, **7**, polarity will be automatically corrected when you align the turnout for the locomotive to leave the reverse loop. All you have to do is get the wires hooked up once with the correct polarity and the auxiliary contacts will take care of it afterward—this can be done by trial and error. This same approach also works for wyes,

but since turntables don't have a switch with auxiliary contacts they require a slightly different approach—more on that in a bit.

What if you use switch machines or manual controls without auxiliary contacts? The best option is an auto-reversing circuit, offered by several manufacturers. An auto reverser wired in line between a booster or DCC power bus and a reverse loop, wye, or turntable will automatically detect a short and reverse track polarity, **12**. These circuits reverse polarity in two different ways: One type uses relays to

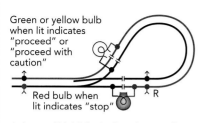

Green or yellow bulb when lit indicates "proceed" or "proceed with caution"

Red bulb when lit indicates "stop"

A. Lamps (16-18V) wired as shown indicate polarity across gaps. Wire across two rails to indicate correct polarity, or along one rail to indicate incorrect polarity.

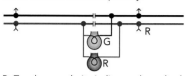

B. Two-lamp polarity indicator shows both correct and incorrect polarity with red and green (or yellow) bulbs

11

A red or green bulb can indicate whether it is safe to enter or leave a reverse loop. You can also wire both a green and red bulb across any rail gaps to indicate whether polarity is correct or not.

12

Independent auto-reversing circuits, like this Digitrax AR1, automatically detect a short circuit and reverse the track polarity.

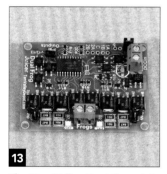

13

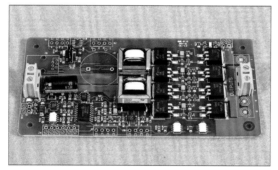

The Tam Valley Dual Frog Juicer configured as an autoreverser, left, can be set for either 2A or 4A. The DCC specialties PSX-AR, right, can be configured to handle current ranging from 1.27A to 17A.

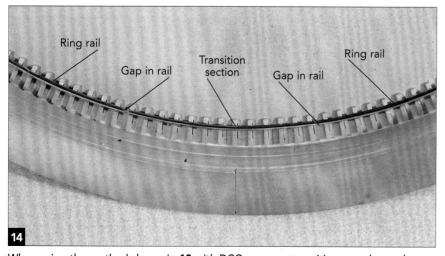

Ring rail

Gap in rail

Transition section

Gap in rail

Ring rail

14

When using the method shown in **10** with DCC power, a transition zone has to be cut into the ring rail and powered through a auto-reversing unit to automatically correct polarity as the turntable rotates.

reverse rail polarity, while the other type uses a solid-state circuit. For users, the difference simply means that solid-state units operate much faster.

Much has been made of this difference in reaction speed by some authors, since it means that the slower units allow for short circuits of longer duration when wheels cross a gap. You can actually see this in some cases by turning off the room lights and watching for a spark at the gap. Some argue that for locomotives in the smaller scales this can severely pit the surfaces of locomotive wheels. I have used auto-reverse units of both designs on my HO layouts and have never noticed pitting, but if you model in N or Z scale then this may be a factor in your decision.

Most auto-reverse units are rated at 5A, so are suitable for use with most scales. The Tam Valley Dual Frog Juicer configured as an auto-reverser can be set for either 2A or 4A, and the DCC Specialties PSX-AR can be configured to handle current ranging from 1.27A to 17A. The PSX-AR also contains a circuit breaker that shuts down power in case of a sustained short that cannot be corrected by auto-reversing track polarity.

Automating turntable polarity with DCC

The easiest way to handle polarity on turntables is to use one of the methods in **7**. You still must manually throw the reversing switch, but that can be automated as well. All three methods in **10** can be automated using the auto-reversing units described earlier. For the methods in **7**, just replace the DPDT switch with an auto reverser and you can forget polarity issues.

If you have a turntable that uses the split-ring rail method, a modification to the ring rail is required. Because DCC power is always present on the track, the two wheels on each bogie create a problem since one will cross the gap ahead of the other creating a short across each bogie. It's necessary to create a transition zone longer than the distance between the two bogie wheels. This transition zone can then be powered through an auto reversing unit to automatically correct polarity as the turntable rotates, **14**. Some commercially available turntables may require modifications, most now come ready for use with DCC. Walthers has even produced one with a DCC decoder already installed for controlling the motor and direction.

Jeff Wilson

CHAPTER EIGHT

Turnout controls

Chapter 4 discussed details of various types of turnouts. When the points of a turnout need to be moved to select a route, we must provide a way to move them and then secure them in that position while the train passes through the turnout. We also need to make sure that the frog is the correct polarity for the chosen route to prevent short circuits. Let's look at ways to manually, mechanically, and electrically control turnouts.

Turnouts can be controlled in a number of ways including manual ground throws and electric under-table switch machines. Ground throws and switch machines alike can also be used to control frog polarity.

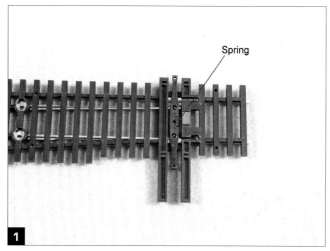

Turnouts made by Micro Engineering and Peco have a small spring mechanism between the points that locks the points into position.

Caboose Industries makes ground throws that resemble the switch stands used on prototype railroads. They are thrown manually by operators.

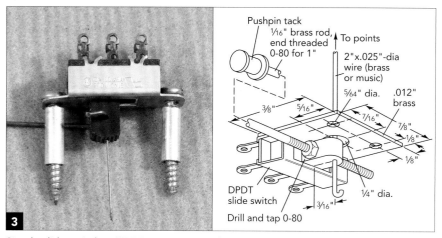

Simple slide switches (SPDT or DPDT) can be mounted under the layout with a piece of piano wire inserted into the plastic slider to throw the turnout points.

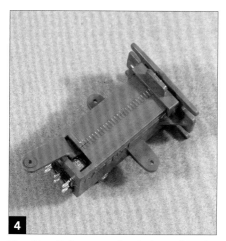

The Blue Point manual switch machine is a clever design that incorporates some features of the popular Tortoise slow-motion machine, with the simple slide switch providing the electrical contacts.

Manual controls

The simplest turnout controls are manual devices. Turnouts made by Micro Engineering and Peco have a small spring mechanism between the points that lock them into position once they have been moved, **1**. These turnouts technically need no other controls, as switching the points can just be done by hand with a finger or a coupler pick.

Most other turnouts have free-moving points that need to be held firmly by a separate control device. Caboose Industries has long offered manually operated ground throws that resemble the switch stands used on prototype railroads, **2**. Although Caboose throws are oversized compared to the real thing, they provide a positive control and

locking mechanism. Caboose also offers versions with built-in electrical switches for controlling frog polarity.

Both of the above approaches have one problem—they require operators to reach into the layout to throw switches. Having operators poking their hands and fingers into a scene is just asking for damage to rolling stock, structures, and scenery. For that and other reasons, I don't have manually controlled turnouts on my layout.

However, there are other relatively inexpensive methods for throwing switches. A simple slide switch (SPDT or DPDT) can be mounted under the layout with a piece of piano wire inserted into the plastic slider to move the points, **3**. A longer metal rod is also inserted into the end of the plastic slider and extended through the layout

edge or fascia to provide a means to move the points. The switch can then be wired to change the frog polarity. I have also seen several variations of this approach with the switch being mounted on the surface of the layout and wires routed under the tracks to control the turnout.

The Blue Point manual switch machine, **4**, is a clever design that incorporates some features of the popular Tortoise slow-motion machine with a simple slide switch providing the electrical contacts.

Electronic controls

Switch machines are devices—usually powered by electricity—that throw turnouts, with control switches (toggle, slide, or push button) located on a control panel, layout fascia, or—for DCC—a handheld cab.

For decades model railroaders depended on solenoid-based switch machines. These consist of two back-to-back electromagnets with a steel rod inserted in a tube running through their core. When current is briefly passed through one electromagnet it pulls the steel rod toward it. If current is then passed through the other electromagnet it pulls the steel rod back in the other direction. This motion—which happens quickly with a "snap"—moves the points.

These were the most popular type of switch machines into the 1980s, when stall-motor machines began gaining in popularity. Many brands of solenoid machines have been offered through the years, with Atlas and Peco still making them. The Atlas N and HO versions, **5** (similar designs were offered by many others over the years), generally require only a small current and can be operated using a low-voltage/low amperage power supply. However, they don't have a lot of torque, so the points have to move freely or they won't move at all.

Peco machines are a bit more robust and are designed to clip to the underside of Peco turnouts, **6**. Peco sells a number of accessories to help install, wire, and operate them. They also come in both a low-amperage version and one that requires a capacitive discharge unit (CDU).

A CDU is an electronic device with a capacitor that can supply a large shot of current to activate larger and more power-hungry twin coil switch machines. Circuitron, for example, makes the Snapper, which can power several large twin-coil switch machines at the same time.

The basic circuit for powering these switch machines uses a SPDT arrangement with one wire from the transformer serving as a common and the other one switched between the two wires leading to the two coils, **7**. A critical feature is that the control switch must be a momentary-contact type. Applying constant power to the

coils will burn them out rather quickly. Atlas makes a special momentary SPDT switch to use with them, **8**.

Kato Unitrack turnouts have a built-in mechanism that uses a reversing 12VDC power-switch circuit to throw the points. Although Kato sells an accessory switch, you can easily make your own using a DPDT momentary-contact switch wired in a reversing configuration.

The most popular switch machines today, especially among experienced modelers, are the slow-motion, stall-motor devices such as the Circuitron Tortoise, **9**, and Smail (a Tortoise with a built-in DCC decoder), Hankscraft SwitchMaster, DCC Concepts Cobalt, and Micro-Mark Switch Tender. They work by having a low-current motor that drives a throw rod. When the points are thrown, the motor stalls, keeping constant pressure on the points. These switch machines generally require a 9-12VDC power supply and only draw about 20 to 60mA when stalled, so a 1A transformer can easily power more than a dozen. To switch the points, the polarity of the motor feeds are simply

reversed using a standard reversing switch or other equally simple methods that can be powered using either a DC or AC power supply, **10**.

The slow motion of the motor produces a prototypically slow movement of the points instead of the rapid snap of the solenoid-based units, which is also easier on turnout components. One advantage the Tortoise and Cobalt machines have over the SwitchMaster and Switch Tender designs is incorporation of two SPDT switches in the mechanism. These switches can be used to control frog polarity, trackside signals, and other devices. Micro-Mark sells a triple-pole, double-throw switch for use with the Switch Tender to both reverse direction of the motor and correct frog polarity when the switch is thrown.

Switching frog polarity

Chapter 4 explained the importance of power-routing turnout frogs to provide continuous power to locomotives passing though them, while at the same time guaranteeing the correct polarity to prevent short circuits. With slow-motion machines that include

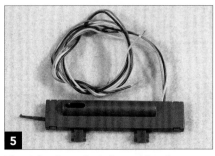

5 The Atlas Snap-Switch machine fits next to the turnout.

6 Peco's solenoid switch machine can be mounted under the layout.

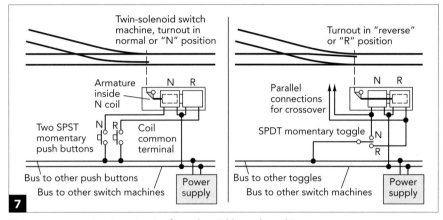

7 Here are two activation circuits for solenoid-based machines.

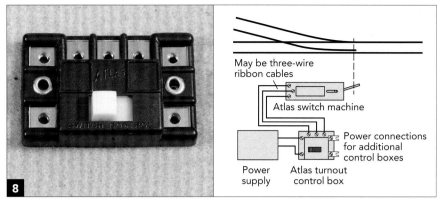

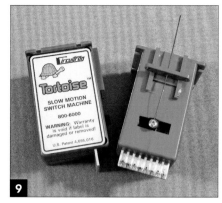

The Atlas switch machine controller is a momentary-contact slide switch. Multiple controllers can be connected together.

The Tortoise stall-motor, under-table switch machine is made by Circuitron.

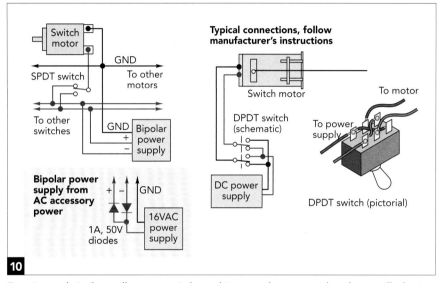

Tortoise and similar stall-motor switch machines can be powered and controlled using either AC or DC using these circuits.

switches and contacts, these can be wired very easily by connecting one wire from each track power bus to the outer contacts of the SPDT switch and then connecting the center contact to the frog, **11**. When the switch machine operates it should route the correct-polarity current to the frog—if it doesn't, then just reverse the two wires from the track power bus and you should be good to go.

Tam Valley Depot makes a specialty circuit board, the Frog Juicer, for use with DCC that automates this process without the use of a switch, **12**. By simply connecting two wires from the track bus to the inputs on the Frog Juicer, and then the output wire to the frog, the device will automatically sense when the polarity is incorrect and switch it for you. The device acts so quickly that boosters will not

shut down due to the momentary short circuit that occurs when the locomotive wheels hit the frog. This can actually have some unexpected consequences—I have run locomotives through the frog of a closed turnout without creating a short, since the Frog Juicer automatically took care of the short circuit, but my locomotive still derailed at the closed switch points! These devices are also great to use with Caboose ground throws that don't have SPDT switches. They come in single-, double-, and six-circuit configurations.

Stationary decoders for DCC

The primary use of stationary decoders is for controlling switch machines. Many companies make stationary decoders for this purpose, and they come in configurations capable of controlling up to eight switch

machines. DCC Specialties' Hare even clips onto the contacts of the Tortoise switch machine, **13**. There are units for use with solenoid-based machines, slow-motion machines, and even one, the NCE SwitchKat, for the Kato Unitrack turnouts. Some units can only control one type of device; others can be programmed for a variety of devices. In addition, Circuiton now offers a version of its Tortoise (the Smail) with a built-in decoder.

Like mobile decoders, stationary decoders are assigned an address. This address can then be used with a throttle or a computer program to tell the decoder to activate a switch machine. Some can only be controlled using a throttle or computer commands, whereas others can also be controlled using switches located on the fascia or a control panel. I prefer the flexibility of also being able to use switches, since it can be difficult for operators to remember the addresses of all the accessory decoders on the layout. This may not be an issue if you only have a few accessory decoders on your layout. You also could place a label on the layout with the decoder address on it, or place the address on the fascia or a control panel. However, I have found that doing this distracts the already-busy engineers.

NCE's Switch8 stationary decoder, which can control eight switch machines, **14**, has an optional circuit board, the Button Board. This device adds the ability to activate each output using momentary push buttons or toggle switches. The Switch8 is a great option for controlling turnout ladders

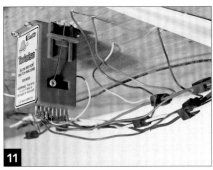

11

A simple way to control frog polarity is to connect one wire from each track power bus (in this case red and green) to the contacts of an SPDT switch on the Tortoise and then connect the yellow output wire to the frog.

12

The Tam Valley Depot Frog Juicer powers the frog and automatically corrects the frog polarity.

13

The DCC Specialties Hare is a stationary decoder that clips onto the contacts of the Tortoise switch machine.

14

NCE's Switch8 stationary decoder, right, can control eight switch machines and has an optional circuit board, the Button Board, left, that adds push button controls.

in yards as well as any area where there are several turnouts.

Setting up routes

If you were a tower operator at a large railroad junction or yard, part of your job would be setting turnouts so that a train could travel through the control area without the crew having to stop and throw each switch along the way. This process is referred to as setting a route for the train.

On our model railroads we can do this by flipping a series of electrical switches to line the turnouts for the desired route. However, model railroaders have come up with many ways to automate this process so that a single control switch can align several turnouts for a given route. One of the oldest methods is the diode matrix.

Because we need to use multiple push buttons to control multiple solenoid coils, we need to prevent current from flowing back along these wires, which could create a situation where both sides of a solenoid are powered at the same time. *Diodes* are semiconductors that allow electrons to flow only in one direction. We can use them to allow current to flow just to the switch machine coils controlling the turnouts we want set for a given route.

As an example, let's look at setting up routes in a yard ladder. The idea is to have one momentary push button for each track in the yard, so that pushing a track's button aligns the turnouts in the ladder that lead to that track. Our example has a compound

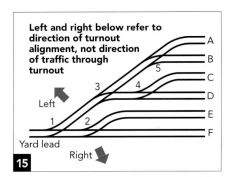

15

This is a compound yard ladder served by five turnouts operated by solenoid switch machines for routes to six tracks.

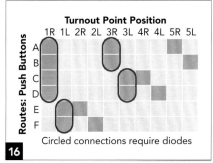

16

This is the diode-matrix planning table for the yard ladder shown in **15**.

yard ladder with five turnouts leading to six individual tracks, **15**. The diodes will be used to control the flow of current when a switch machine is connected to multiple push buttons.

To simplify the planning process, we can set up a table with turnout positions across the top and the push buttons for the routes listed along the left side, **16**. Note that left or right refers to the *direction the points must be thrown*. Next we color in each box for each turnout position required for each route. For example, route A requires that turnout 1 be set to the right (1R),

turnout 3 be set to the right (3R), and turnout 5 be set to the right (5R). In each turnout column, circle any group of two or more filled-in boxes. You'll need a diode in the wire from each push button to the solenoid control wire for that turnout position. The final diagram is shown in **17**. Diodes are shown in the diagram as an arrowhead with a line across the tip of it—the line represents the end of the diode with a white band on it. A common 1N4001 diode will work well.

The problem with this diode-matrix approach is that it only works with

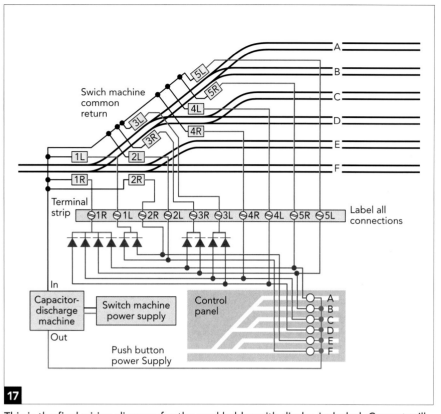

17

This is the final wiring diagram for the yard ladder with diodes included. Current will only flow in the direction of the arrows representing the diodes and will be blocked from taking additional paths back through the wires.

solenoid switch machines—some fancy wiring is required when using Tortoises and other stall-motor switch machines.

Many circuits have appeared in *Model Railroader* showing methods for setting up routes. One I particularly like appeared in the November 2000 issue. Designed by David Smith, the basic design uses an asymmetric split-voltage approach with a rotary switch to select the routes. Normally each Tortoise in the ladder receives positive polarity from the +18V supply through a dropping resistor. When the rotary switch is set to a particular turnout, negative polarity at -9V is routed to it, reversing the switch machine, **18**. You can see a more-complex track circuit using David's method in **19**. A parts list for these circuits is provided in **20**.

An article in the May 2009 MR by Oliver Tansey provides another approach for stall-motor route control. His method uses SPDT switches built into the Tortoise switch machine and 560-ohm, 1-watt resistors to set up the routes, which also are selected using a rotary switch, **20**.

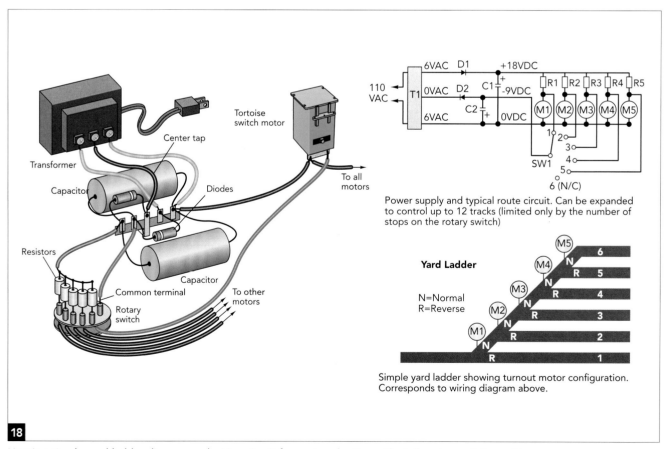

Power supply and typical route circuit. Can be expanded to control up to 12 tracks (limited only by the number of stops on the rotary switch)

Yard Ladder

N=Normal
R=Reverse

Simple yard ladder showing turnout motor configuration. Corresponds to wiring diagram above.

18

Here's a simple yard ladder diagram and wiring circuit for route selection with stall-motor switch machines.

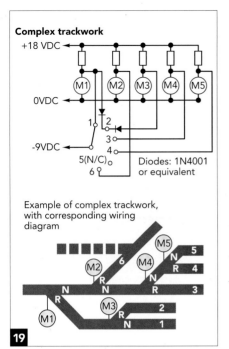

19

This is a more complex example of a track diagram and wiring circuit for route selection with stall-motor machines.

DCC stationary decoders

Stationary decoders like the NCE Switch8 and the Digitrax DS64 have an important feature: the ability to program them for routes. Just like the diode-matrix approach, you can have a momentary SPST switch for each route that serves as an input to the accessory decoder, telling it to align the series of turnouts for each of those routes. Setting up routes in accessory decoders requires some planning and programming. These steps vary among manufacturers and units, so—although not difficult—going into detail is beyond the scope of this book, and most manufacturers provide good tutorials on the process. To get an idea of what is involved, manuals and tutorials can be downloaded from their websites.

It may take a few minutes to program a decoder for all possible routes, but it is less time-consuming than setting up and installing a diode matrix control system. As I will discuss in Chapter 12, you can also set up routes using computer programs like JMRI PanelPro, creating a virtual CTC board that your dispatcher can use to remotely throw switches all over your layout just like on the prototype.

20. Parts list for David Smith's control circuit

T1	273-1352	"12.6V, 1.2A center-tap transformer"
"D1, D2"	275-1101	1N4001 diode
"C1, C2"	272-1022	4700uF electrolytic capacitor
R1-Rm	271-1121	"2.2k ohm, 1/2-watt resistor"
SW1	101532	"12 position, 1 pole rotary switch"
M1-Mn		Tortoise switch machine
Knob	274-407	Knob
TS	274-688	Terminal strip

Note: all part numbers are Radio Shack except SW1 which is Jameco

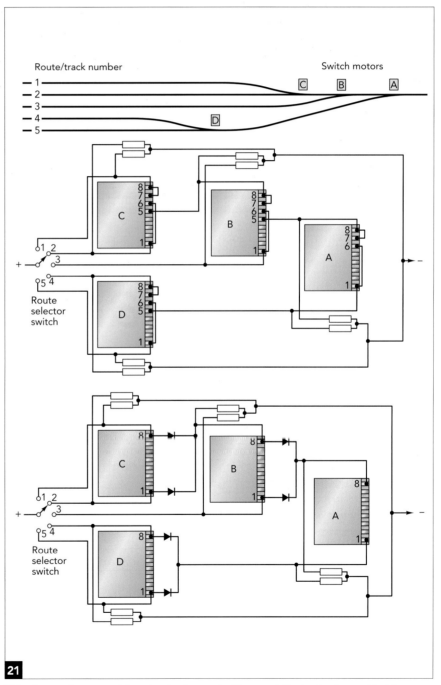

21

This shows alternate wiring circuits for controlling a relatively simple yard ladder using stall-motor switch machines. The resistors shown are 560-ohm, 1-watt, assuming a 12VDC power supply.

Jeff Wilson

CHAPTER NINE

Control panels

This control panel, mounted to the layout's fascia, holds the rotary switches and push buttons that control turnouts at one end of a large yard. The track schematic, including lettering, is printed on paper and then covered by clear acrylic sheet that's screwed in place. This panel is on Kalmbach's Milwaukee, Racine & Troy HO club layout.

For much of the history of model railroading, modelers built large control panels to operate their model railroads. A typical panel consisted of a large diagram of the track plan painted on plywood or hardboard, with block control switches located on the track plan allowing operators to route power from their cabs to specific blocks.

There would also be switches on the track plan to control turnouts and reverse loops and wyes. Engineers typically sat in one location with their throttles/power packs.

As walkaround operation increased in popularity beginning in the 1970s and '80s, centralized control panels began to disappear, replaced by smaller local panels scattered around the layout. These allow engineers to route power and switch turnouts as they follow their trains. With the smaller panels it also became popular to recess controls into the layout fascia, where they would be handy yet out of the way as engineers walked through the aisles.

Today there are a number of different ways to control a model railroad, and whether you even use control panels depends to a large degree on whether you use DC cab control or DCC. With DC cab control, a control panel provides a full or partial diagram of the layout with switches placed on it to control each block (see photos on pages 36 and 39).

However, with DCC you only need switches to control turnouts, and you don't even need these if you use manual controls or stationary decoders—once again, DCC can make things a lot simpler and easier. I regularly operate on a large DCC layout that doesn't have any panels to control turnouts—with the exception of a few slow-motion switch machines for turnouts in remote locations, all the turnouts are controlled with Caboose Industries ground throws.

One popular alternative to control panels is to paint small sections of the track plan directly on the fascia in front of the section of track depicted. Small toggle switches can then be installed on the fascia for turnout control. If there is only one turnout in a given location you don't even need the track diagram—just mount the switch on the fascia in front of the turnout. One trick is to drill a hole in the fascia and mount the switch in the recess to protect it from accidental bumping damage as your operators follow their trains around the layout, **1**.

You can also mount controls for various other accessories in the fascia.

1 Drill a hole in the fascia and mount the switch on a board in the recess to protect it.

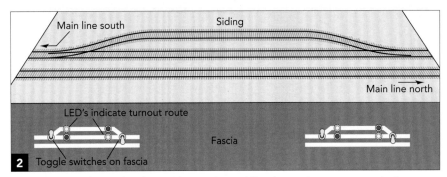

2 On my HO Piedmont Southern, I have a long siding located on an upper deck over a busy yard. To aid operators, I installed dual turnout control panels on the fascia.

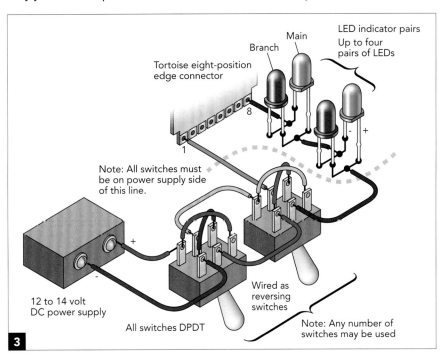

3 Wiring Tortoise switch machines using DPDT reversing switches and pairs of LEDs allows control of the turnouts from opposite ends of the siding. The LEDs are installed in a fascia diagram to indicate which way the turnouts are aligned.

For example, I use momentary-contact switches that activate electromagnetic uncouplers at various places on my layout. I also have the controls for my Boulder Creek Engineering track scales mounted in the fascia. The really important reasons for this approach instead of a centralized control panel are that it's more compatible with walkaround operations and it is easier for operators to find the control switches they need.

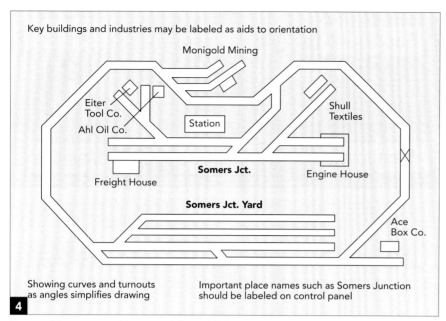

Key buildings and industries may be labeled as aids to orientation

Monigold Mining

Eiter Tool Co.

Ahl Oil Co.

Station

Shull Textiles

Somers Jct.

Engine House

Freight House

Somers Jct. Yard

Ace Box Co.

Showing curves and turnouts as angles simplifies drawing

Important place names such as Somers Junction should be labeled on control panel

4

For small layouts, a schematic of the model railroad may be a good approach.

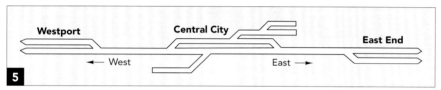

Westport

Central City

East End

← West

East →

5

Straight-line diagrams fit easily on the layout's fascia.

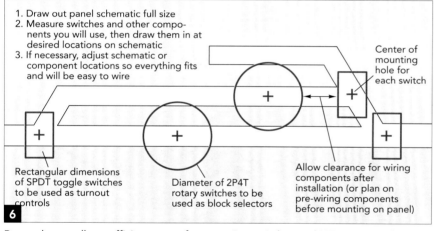

1. Draw out panel schematic full size
2. Measure switches and other components you will use, then draw them in at desired locations on schematic
3. If necessary, adjust schematic or component locations so everything fits and will be easy to wire

Center of mounting hole for each switch

Rectangular dimensions of SPDT toggle switches to be used as turnout controls

Diameter of 2P4T rotary switches to be used as block selectors

Allow clearance for wiring components after installation (or plan on pre-wiring components before mounting on panel)

6

Remember to allow sufficient space for mounting switches and LEDs in your diagram.

Locations

As you design your model railroad and plan how to operate it, give some thought to where you might want to put control panels. Let's assume you want to use switch machines to control your turnouts on a large DCC layout. In areas with a lot of tracks, such as a yard or industrial switching area such as the one shown on page 68, it's handy to have a schematic-based control panel with switches to control all those turnouts.

For less-complex areas, where you only have one or a few turnouts, all you need is a switch on the fascia to control them, perhaps with labels as in **1**. Basically, if the diagram and switches will fit on your fascia, then that will do.

For example, on my Piedmont Southern I have a small yard panel for Charlottesville, Va. Because the industrial switching area next to the yard is set back about a foot and located over another industrial switching area on the lower deck, I can't mount control

switches on the fascia. So I placed the controls for those turnouts on the small yard panel. This works well with my operating scheme since the yard crew is responsible for switching the industries in this area. However, occasionally your diagram may be too big to fit on the fascia in which case you will need to add a small panel to it.

Another consideration is the size requirements for large control panels mounted on the fascia. Depending on the height of the layout, the panel might need to be angled upward for good visibility. Thus a panel located 54" above the floor may be mounted flush with the fascia or have the bottom extend out an inch or two, whereas the bottom of the same panel at 42" may have to extend outward several inches. For tight aisles there are other options, such as suspending the panel from the ceiling (which can cause problems for modelers of different heights) or, a better idea, recessing it into the fascia as Jim Hediger did for his staging-yard panel shown on page 36.

Most turnouts are controlled with a single switch mounted in the fascia or panel. However, at times it's desirable to control a turnout from multiple locations. On my Piedmont Southern I have a long siding located on my upper deck over a busy yard, **2**. Since I don't want my train crew working the upper deck bumping into the yard crew working in the middle of the yard below, I installed duplicate switches to control each turnout. The duplicate switches were installed in duplicate diagrams on the fascia at opposite ends of the upper deck, straddling the lower yard. The same technique can be used to provide duplicate controls for turnouts at a dispatcher's panel.

Wiring each switch requires only a couple of simple DPDT reversing switches, **3**, wired in line. To serve as an indication of which way the turnouts are aligned, I installed a pair of LEDs in the fascia track plan at each switch position. The corresponding LED illuminates to indicate the selected route. If after installing them they light up incorrectly, just reverse their wiring—remember that the longer leg of an LED is positive.

Design and construction

Control panels can be designed as an exact replica of the layout, **4**, which may be a good choice for a small layout. However, the same layout could be represented as straight-line segments, **5**. Straight-line segments also work well for laying out yard schematics on a panel or placing a small segment of a track plan on the fascia, **6**. As you design the track plan, don't forget to plan locations and allow space for switches and LEDs, **6**. The level of detail on a schematic will depend to a large part on how wide the fascia is. Obviously a large yard diagram (page 68) won't fit on a 3"-wide fascia, but the narrower track schematic in **5** will.

For a simple fascia diagram I first paint that area of the fascia a light color such as white, ivory, or yellow. Next I use thin striping tape, available at auto and office supply stores, to lay out the track diagram. You can also cut long strips of masking tape. Finally I paint on a dark color and immediately remove the tape—the longer you leave it on the more likely it is to pull off the paint underneath. You can then drill holes for mounting components and install the switches and LEDs. See Appendix A to see how it's done.

Another approach is to lay out your track diagram using a computer graphics program, print out a color version, and attach it to the fascia, **7**. If you want to protect it, cover it with a thin sheet of adhesive plastic film or

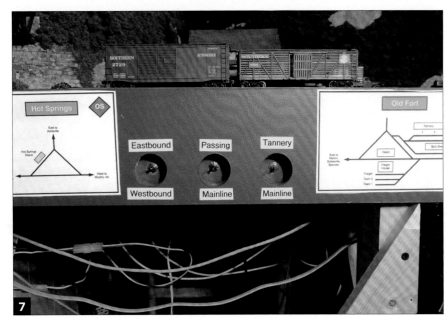

Computer-generated plans can simply be printed out and glued to the fascia.

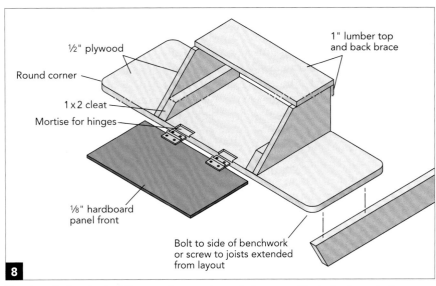

Here's a design for building small control panels for use with dual-cab control.

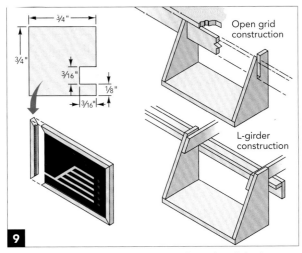

Control panels can be attached to the side of the layout. They can be angled for better visibility.

One of my older fascia-mounted panels includes the schematic and switches along with customized lettering.

11

12

This large panel controls most of a medium-size layout.

Hinges allow the panel to open for access to the wiring.

clear acrylic (such as Plexiglas), then drill and mount the switches. I like this method a lot since it protects your diagram and makes it easy to change or replace them as needed. Most copy shops can laminate these diagrams for a reasonable fee.

For small control panels like my Charlottesville, Va., yard, I treat it like a fascia panel. I make the panel itself out of thin plywood or tempered hardboard and either paint the track diagram on it as described above or create it in a graphics program and print out a color version. I then install the Plexiglas cover, mark and drill the holes for switches, and finally mount and wire everything. Making the panel hinged at the top or bottom allows it to be flipped open for easy access to the wiring and components. You can see a design for building control panels for use with dual-cab control in **8**.

There are alternative designs for small fascia-mounted panels that

can be attached to L-girders or open frame components, **9**. I have used a similar design in the past for control panels that I attached to the fascia, **10**. More elaborate and larger control panels can be built using the same plan, **11**, with hinges allowing the panel to tip out for access to wiring, **12**.

Adding lights and switches

On some of my panels I have added lights to the track plan to help engineers follow the route and throw the correct switches. I mount LEDs in special fixtures designed for that purpose in small holes drilled in the plan, **13**. By wiring the LEDs in line with the Tortoise switch machines, **3**, the correct LED will illuminate, showing which leg of the turnout the points are set for. Because of the low current draw of the Tortoise motor, you don't even need a resistor in the wiring for the LEDs. These could also be used on fascia installations but are best used

in areas of complex track routes.

Another useful addition to control panels are switches to kill power to certain tracks where you may want to store locomotives when not in use. These kill switches help lengthen decoder life, guarantee that an unattended locomotive won't drift off if inadvertently left on speed step 1, and—since sound decoders are cut off—reduce the noise level in the train room. A simple SPST switch wired into one track feeder is all that is required to turn power on and off to that track.

Push buttons for accessory decoders

Accessory decoders are great if you want to use a computer system to automate parts of your operations or to create a virtual Centralized Traffic Control (CTC) board allowing your dispatcher to remotely control turnouts (more on that in Chapter 12). However, as discussed in Chapter 8, accessory decoders are also useful for setting up routes in complex sections of track like yard ladders.

Using accessory decoders like the Switch8 and its Button Board or the Digitrax DS64, **14**, you can set up routes that are activated using push buttons mounted on the control panel. A simple momentary SPST switch is all that's required to serve as an input to activate these devices. Drill a mounting hole, install the switch, run the wires to the device, and you have a reliable way to control complex turnout installations.

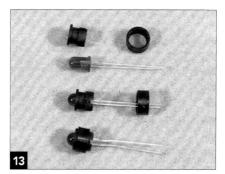

13

These small mounting fixtures allow LEDs to be easily installed in a control panel.

14

The NCE Switch8 and its Button Board and the Digitrax DS64 accessory decoders can be programmed to select routes using momentary push buttons on the control panel or fascia.

Andy Sperandeo

CHAPTER TEN

Layout wiring

Regardless of whether you're using DC or DCC, the importance of wiring your layout properly remains the same. Taking shortcuts in the number of feeders or rushing through soldering might save a bit of money and time, but your layout will suffer in poor operation—and it's no fun trying to trace a stray short circuit or wire failure. Wires need to be of the proper size and type, connections need to be solid and electrically reliable, and track feeders must be securely soldered to do the job.

Keeping wiring neat—color coding wires, organizing bus wires, and labeling wires—makes the job easier and will aid in any necessary troubleshooting later. This is Andy Sperandeo's HO scale Santa Fe layout.

Types of wire

There are 2 basic types of wire: solid and stranded, **1**. As the name implies, stranded wire is made up of a number of smaller wires (strands) and can take a lot of flexing without breaking. It therefore is useful for connections on modular layouts that get moved around a lot, as well as in control panels that slide, flip, or otherwise move. Another place to use stranded wire is for the small wires used to provide power to accessories such as lights, animated features, sound boards, and other electronic devices. Its flexibility can make it easier to work into buildings and out-of-the-way places. Finally, these small wires usually end up getting moved a lot when you are working under the layout and their flexibility can help prevent breakage.

Solid wire is stiff and best suited for situations where there will be little flexing required. If flexed at one spot too often, solid wire can eventually break, creating intermittent or permanent power interruptions that are difficult to locate. Fortunately on model railroads most heavy wiring is subjected to very little movement, so solid wire is useful for main track/power buses, track feeders, and accessory buses.

As with track, wire size is a very important consideration when wiring your layout. Wire size is measured by gauge, following American Wire Gauge (AWG) standards. The higher the number, the lighter (smaller

1 Solid wire is stiff and doesn't flex very well, but it's good for heavy power buses. Stranded wire is made up of multiple small wires and is flexible, making it a good choice for wires that will be moved a lot.

2. Voltage drop per foot for various-sized wire at 1 amp and 5 amps

Wire gauge	1A	5A
12	0.003	0.016
14	0.005	0.025
18	0.013	0.064
20	0.02	0.1
22	0.032	0.16

Note: all are 1-way values and would double for out and back runs.

Recommended power bus wire sizes

Scale	Wire gauge
O	10-12
HO, S	12-16
N-Z	16-18

In general, the heavier the wire, the lower the voltage drop; the more current that needs to pass through the bus, the heavier the wire needs to be.

3 To help minimize voltage drops along rails I solder most rail joiners at joints (left). To allow for expansion and contraction, I leave some rail joiners unsoldered (right) and make feeders supply all rails.

4. Voltage drop per foot of various sizes of nickel silver rail at 1 amp and 5 amps

Rail code	1A	5A
100	0.056	0.28
83	0.085	0.42
70	0.152	0.76
55	0.22	1.11

As this chart shows, nickel silver rail is a poor electrical conductor compared to copper wire. This problem is made worse with smaller rail sizes, which can see a significant voltage drop over even a foot or two of rail length. Rail code is the height of rail in thousandths of an inch (code 83 rail is .083" tall). Note that rail codes apply regardless of scale—for example, the voltage drop applies equally with code 55 HO rail and code 55 N scale rail.

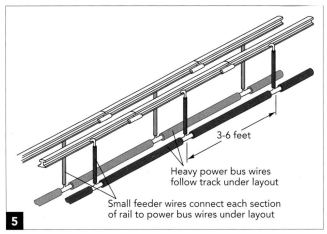

Depending on the code of your track, install power feeders every three to six feet—use more feeders for smaller rail.

diameter) the wire; the lower the number, the heaver the wire. As an example, 22-gauge (or 22AWG) wire is fairly light and typically used for track feeders; 14-gauge wire is heavier and suitable for many power buses.

A general rule is that the more current that will be passing through the wire, the heavier it has to be. This brings up an important difference in wiring a conventional DC layout versus a DCC-controlled model railroad. On a conventional DC layout it is unlikely that there will be more than 1 to 1.5 amps passing through the main feeder wires, whereas on a DCC power bus this may reach 5A to 10A. Also with DCC, even though typical useage may only max out at 1.5A or so for a group of locomotives while running, during a short circuit the entire 5 to 10 amps will be coursing through the wires and rails.

To prevent voltage drops—which can happen if wire is not heavy enough for the load—and insure that your booster or other short-circuit protection devices work properly, plan and wire for the worst-case scenario, not just the typical operating condition.

The goal, therefore, is to have heavy enough wires to prevent significant drops in voltage. This is proportional to the amperage of the current being transmitted and the length of the wire run. There are many websites that will calculate the voltage drop for a given gauge of wire and amperage. The table in **2** shows guidelines from www.calculator.net. As you can see, with heavy wires you only run into problems on very long runs. The problem comes with the much smaller feeder wires. Because of their smaller diameters, resistance is much greater and can reduce track voltage. Consequently, I

recommend keeping feeders less than three feet long and using either 22- or 20-gauge solid wire, although you may need to go as high as 16-gauge wire in O and S scales.

When installing main power buses on DC layouts, **2**, I suggest 12- to 16-gauge wire for HO and S scales, 16- to 18-gauge for N and Z scales, and 10- or 12-gauge wire for O scale. These recommendations are for typical bus lengths and current loads, so on runs over 30 feet it may be necessary to step up to the next larger size of wire.

As an example, I'm aware of at least one HO layout with buses over 100 feet long where 10-gauge wire is used. If you are running similarly long buses on an N scale layout with 5A boosters, consider stepping up to the larger gauge wire recommended for HO layouts.

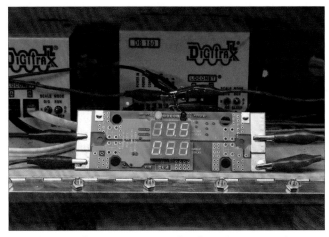

The DCC Specialties RRampmeter can be used to measure DCC track voltage and amperage. Note that for voltage it can be used anywhere, but for amperage measurements it must be wired in line with the feeder wires going to the track.

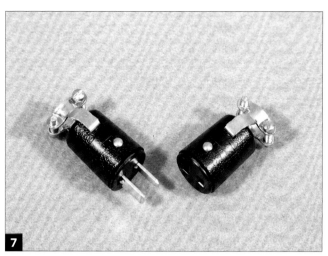

7

Cinch-Jones plugs are common for connecting wiring, especially on modular layouts, but they create enough resistance to significantly reduce track voltage.

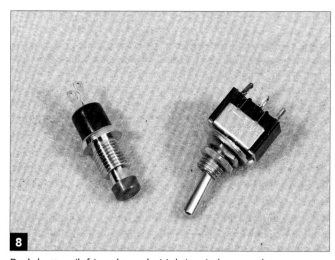

8

Push button (left) and toggle (right) switches are the most common electrical switches used on model railroads. They are available in many configurations.

Track

Chapter 1 mentions that track comes in different materials and sizes. Both factors affect electrical resistance. For efficient operation, we need to limit any drop in voltage due to track resistance as much as possible. This is especially critical with DCC, since a drop in track voltage of just a few volts can degrade control, meaning booster circuitry might have difficulty detecting when a short occurs.

Track connections are a major concern as well, because unsoldered rail-joiner connections can be a major reason for voltage drops. To solve this I typically solder rail joiners between most (but not all) sections of track, **3**. Leave some joints unsoldered with small rail gaps to allow for expansion and contraction of layout materials as humidity and temperature fluctuate in your train room.

How much voltage loss can you expect from different sizes of track? Table **4** shows voltage drops for various sizes of nickel-silver track. You can see that you stand to lose a lot more voltage in your track than in your wires. It gets even worse when you consider that the values in the chart are only for one rail—they double when you figure that there are two rails in track. To avoid these potentially large voltage drops, increase the frequency of feeders between the main power bus and the rails, **5**. On my HO layout I use feeders every six feet for my code 83 track and

every four feet for my code 70 track. For HO and N modelers with code 55 rail I recommend placing feeders at least every three feet. The bottom line: To reduce voltage drops you need to use the proper size wire for your main power buses, keep your feeders as short as possible, and place your feeders close enough together.

How can you tell whether your track wiring is adequate? For standard DC, a good start is to use a multimeter to check the voltage at various points along the track in each block. As you run trains, if you notice locomotives slowing down in certain spots, it might be wise to add additional feeders.

With DCC, the cheap and easy method is to lay a coin on the track. If your short-circuit warning fails to sound, then your track and wire resistance is too great. But what if you actually want to measure your track voltage? Unfortunately, DCC track-voltage frequencies are too high to measure directly using a standard voltmeter. DCC Specialties makes the RRampmeter, which measures both voltage and amperage of the DCC circuit. For voltage measurements you simply place its contacts on the rails anywhere on the layout, **6**, but make sure you have a load on the rails such as a light bulb or a locomotive. To measure the amperage being used on the track, the RRampmeter must be wired in the power bus between the booster and the track. Although it can

be used as a portable voltmeter, you can also install the RRampmeter into your layout fascia, a control panel, or command station/booster shelf to constantly monitor the voltage and amperage used.

Modular layouts

Modular layouts have become very popular, but they present some particular problems with respect to wire and track voltage drops, especially in N scale. Modules are commonly daisy-chained using small-diameter wires connected together with Cinch-Jones or similar connectors, **7**. Add to that the fact that N scale track is either code 80 or code 55 and you can see the potential problems, especially with DCC. Cinch-Jones plugs in particular can greatly contribute to voltage drops. A friend of mine once measured voltage drops on his N scale modules with and without Cinch-Jones connectors, and he discovered the connectors accounted for a third of the drop in voltage alone.

To avoid this problem, while still allowing modules using Cinch Jones plugs to operate as part of N scale gatherings, I suggest that a main power bus be used consisting of 12- to 14-gauge wires with 18-gauge drops spliced in at about eight-foot intervals. By attaching a male Cinch-Jones plug to the end of these drops it would be possible to attach every other module directly to the main power bus.

9

10

A single-pole, single-throw (SPST) switch, left, only has one pair of contacts. It is typically used to interrupt the flow of electricity in a single wire. A double-pole, double-throw (DPDT) switch, right, has two sets of contacts and two possible routes allowing it to route power to two different sets of tracks or circuits.

The center-off position on this DPDT switch provides an electrically dead position. It prevents short circuits from occurring as the switch is thrown.

Switches

Model railroaders use a number of different types of electrical switches. Most are of two basic types: push button and toggle, **8**. Push button switches can be the momentary-contact type in a normally on or normally off configuration, or can be an on-off type. Normally off momentary switches are handy for circuits like accessory decoders that are designed for a brief contact to turn them on, or where you only want something to operate while you hold down the button, such as a solenoid-type switch machine. Normally on switches are for circuits that require power to be on all the time but can be briefly turned off by holding down the pushbutton. On-off switches simply turn power on and then off each time you push them.

Toggle switches are probably the most-common variety and come in several configurations. These are named based on the number of poles they have and the number of contacts they make, **9**. The poles refer to the number of wires they control—a single pole controls one wire whereas a double pole controls two wires.

The typical on/off light switch in your home is likely a single-pole, single-throw switch (SPST). Single-pole, double-throw (SPDT) switches can be used to route power to two different paths or to selectively connect two different wires to one path. This type switch is commonly used to route the correct polarity power to an isolated frog.

A double-pole, single-throw (DPST) switch controls two wires in a circuit and turns it on or off—it simply makes or breaks both wires of the circuit. This could be used to cut off both wires powering a section of track. A double-pole, double-throw (DPDT) switch controls two wires and can connect them to two different circuits or connect two different pairs of wires to one circuit or device. These are also used to make reversing switches.

Many toggles are offered in a make-break-make configuration which isolates the two poles as they are thrown, helping to prevent intermittent shorts, **10**. Some also have a center-off position, which is useful in a two-cab DC control setup so that blocks not in use are not powered.

There are a number of specialty switches such as multi-position rotary switches that allow you to select a circuit by rotating the control knob, **11**. These can be used to route power to a track in a staging yard or to select which cab controls a block in a multi-cab DC setup.

Connectors

I like to solder every connection possible—I am very leery of using any type of electrical connection that is not soldered. For example, slip-fit rail joiners are susceptible to oxidation, dirt, grease, oil, paint, and scenery cement. These kinds of contamination easily find their way into joints, all of which can lead to a loss of electrical continuity. None of these things will affect a soldered joint.

However, there are always situations where it isn't desirable or possible to use a soldered connection. Many accessories on and under the layout over time may fail and need to be replaced. There are also places on the layout where we may need to periodically disconnect sections of track for maintenance, removal, or troubleshooting. In these locations there are several types of connectors that will do the job.

Tie strips, **12**, have been around for decades and consist of a piece of phenolic board with several metal strips riveted to it. A wire from the power supply can be soldered to one prong on the strip and then wires to lights and other accessories can be soldered to the other prongs. For a large number of accessory wires you can daisy-chain the prongs and have one strip for the positive wire and another for the negative or ground wire. Disconnecting a wire is as easy as touching the solder joint with a hot soldering iron.

Screw-type terminal strips and

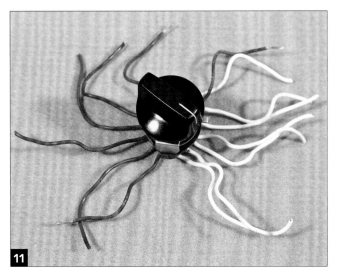

11 Rotary switches allow you to select from a number of possible circuit paths. These can be useful for controlling a number of switch machines or to route power to a series of yard tracks.

12 Tie strips provide a way to attach several wires to a single circuit or power source by simply soldering them all to the metal posts.

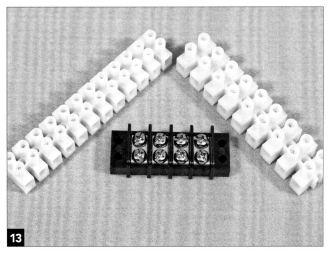

13 Terminal strips and terminal blocks allow for quick and easy screw connections.

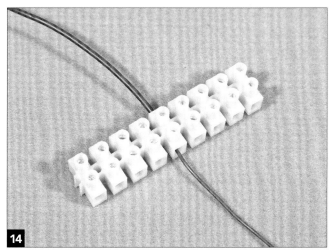

14 Terminal blocks are great for connecting two wires of different sizes together. The screws provide a strong grip on the wires.

terminal blocks, **13**, make removing connections even easier. Terminal blocks consist of a nylon block with several metal channels into which the two wires to be connected are inserted and clamped down with screws. They are especially good for joining large wires. For example, I use them to connect a short section of 14-gauge stranded wire from my power supply to the 12- and 14-gauge solid copper main bus wires, **14**. Another useful application is for joining the bus wires at lift-out sections.

Screw-type terminals usually have two rows of screws connected by metal strips which pass current from the supply wire to the accessory wire. A bare wire can be wrapped around the screw which is tightened down to give a good electrical connection. Several of these can be daisy chained using jumpers, **15**, so that only one positive and negative bus connection is required. Some folks like to use crimped spade connectors on the end of the wires for an even neater installation, **16**.

Several types of crimped connectors are available. These typically consist of a metal tube in a plastic sleeve into which the two wires to be joined are inserted and then the metal sleeve is crimped tight on them, making a firm electrical connection, **17**. The two types I find most useful are those with a closed end and those open on both ends. Either type gives a strong and reliable electrical connection for extending wires. Inexpensive crimping tools, **18**, make connections fast and reliable.

A potential problem with using these is that over time the wires can oxidize, resulting in loss of continuity. To prevent this I like to use Ox-Gard, a brand of anti-oxidant grease. This product is a grease containing zinc and graphite, making it electrically conductive. When applied to a joint and the wires pressed together, the grease is displaced leaving an electrically conductive zinc-and-graphite layer between the wire surfaces. The grease around the wires prevents future corrosion and also makes the joint moisture resistant.

Screw terminals can be used with individual wires or with a jumper to connect to multiple wires.

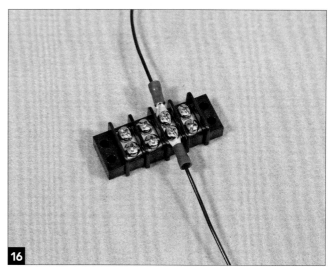

Crimped spade connectors make for fast and neat installations.

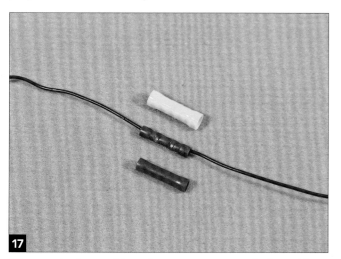

Wires can be inserted into sleeve connectors and crimped for a reliable solderless connection.

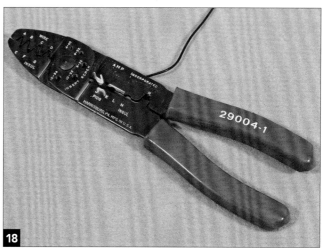

This inexpensive tool makes it easy to add crimp connectors to wires.

Suitcase connectors

3M and others make several types of insulation displacement connectors (IDCs), more popularly known as suitcase connectors, **19**. The basic design is similar—a metal blade with two slits in it is held firmly in a plastic case. The wires to be joined are fed into openings in the case which align them with the slits. When the metal blade is pressed down using pliers or a special crimping tool, the slits in the metal blade close down over the wires, displacing the insulation and cutting into the sides of the wires. This provides a solid electrical connection.

One thing to keep in mind is that the slits in the blade are sized for the wire diameters specified and should not be use with other wire sizes, as they will either cut too deeply or not deeply enough into other wires.

Suitcase connectors are designed for low voltage—32 volts or less. They are popular for automotive applications, and model railroaders began using them about 20 years ago. They are available for either splicing wires of similar sizes or for wires of significantly different diameters. The ones in **20** look very much alike but the one on the left in the photo is for splicing two wires in the 18- to 22-gauge range, whereas the one on the right is designed to connect a 14- to 18-gauge bus to an 18- to 22-gauge tap or feeder. I use the first one to connect accessories to a 12VDC bus. The other one, a 3M no. 905, is perfect for connecting 22-gauge track feeders to a 14-gauge power bus.

For large (10-12-gauge) bus wires, 3M makes the no. 558 connector with a dual blade. I purchase the 3M 905 from Mouser, and All Electronics offers two sizes of the quick-splice connectors.

Suitcase connectors allow you to wire the track feeders for a whole model railroad in a fraction of the time it would take to solder even a few feeders to a bus wire. To install one, place the run wire in the channel with two openings and the tap wire into the channel with one opening, **21**. Press the metal piece in place using either pliers or a tool designed for this. I have used Vise-Grip pliers for almost 20 years to clamp them down, **22**. Make sure the suitcase latch clips down over the bottom of the case with

79

19

Suitcase connectors, or insulation-displacement connectors (IDCs), have a very simple design and are easy to use for installing feeders to main power buses.

20

These two connectors look almost alike, but the one on the left is for splicing two 18- to 22-gauge wires and the one on the right is to connect a 14- to 18-gauge bus to an 18- to 24-gauge tap or feeder.

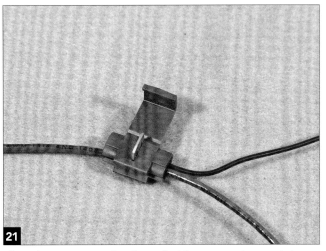

21

Place the run wire in the channel with two openings and the tap wire into the channel with one opening.

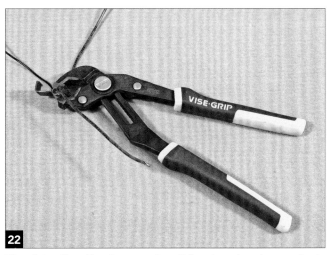

22

Vise-Grip pliers like these work well for clamping the metal tab down to complete the connection.

a click, and it's done. Always check electrical continuity of the feeder or spliced wires before hooking them up to the rails or the accessory to be powered—sometimes it is necessary to go back and give the device a few more crimps with the pliers to get a tight connection.

Organization

Many model railroads end up with a large number of wires running in all directions under the layout. Without some type of organization and record keeping, you can later end up spending hours troubleshooting even the simplest problems.

The first step is to develop a system of color codes for your wires. For

example, on my double-track layout I use red wires for powering the rails of each track closest to the aisle and green wires for the rails away from the aisle. I use yellow wires for the feeders to frogs, and white and black wires for the 12VDC accessory power bus. When running long power buses to different blocks, I tie the red and green wires for each block together at eight-foot intervals, **23**.

Some DCC manufacturers recommend twisting power bus wires together about three turns per foot, especially if the run is 30 feet or longer, to reduce interference caused by inductance. This is known as a *twisted pair*, and it can overcome a number of issues with long runs including signal

degradation, electronic noise, and voltage spikes which can kill decoders. For very long runs, some manufacturers now recommend adding a terminating resistor and capacitor at the end of the bus wires (see Chapter 3), but check with your system manual or call your manufacturer's technical support line if in doubt.

Some modelers like to run a 120VAC line under the layout with outlets built into the front of the layout. This makes it handier to connect to an AC source, especially under a fully scenicked and built layout. However, if you do this make sure your work meets local building codes and passes local inspections. At a minimum, metal shielded cable should

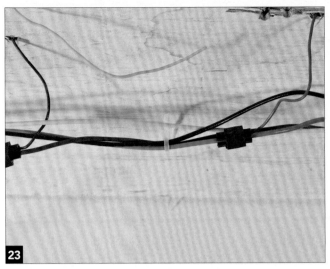

23 On my power buses I tie the wires for each block together at six- to eight-foot intervals.

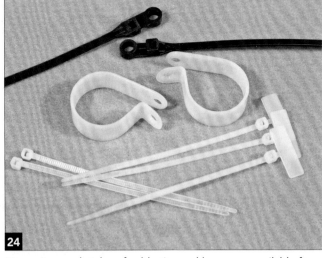

24 Many sizes and styles of cable ties and loops are available for organizing wiring.

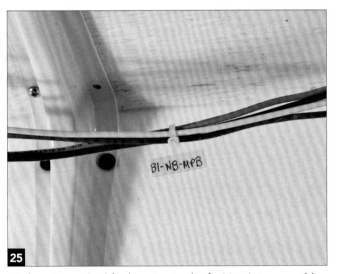

25 My favorite method for keeping track of wiring is to use cable ties with a tag end to label the wire bundle.

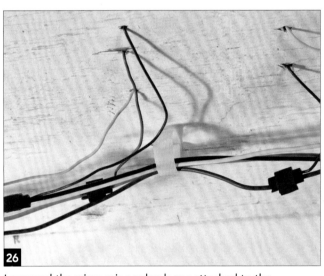

26 I suspend the wires using nylon loops attached to the underside of the layout.

be used so that you and your crew don't accidentally cut into a live 120VAC wire.

There are catalogs full of products for bundling wires. Some folks use plastic-coated wire strips like those on bread loaves. Others prefer nylon or plastic twist locks, clamps, cable ties, or hook and loop strips, **24**. I have been using cable ties on my current layout to bundle wires and am very happy with the results, **25**. Some plastic ties are available with mounting holes molded into them that allow you to attach them to the underside of the layout using a wood screw.

Wires can be run through holes drilled in the layout joists or through plastic or nylon loops attached to

the underside of the layout—you can also use cup hooks. I run my bundled cables through nylon loops attached to the underside of the layout, **26**. I like the nylon loops since wire will slide easily through them and they can be moved by simply backing out the screw and screwing it in elsewhere. I do recommend using different loops or holes for different types of buses.

Electronic noise becomes an issue if throttle and booster network wiring is located adjacent to power buses. I recommend providing anywhere from 6" to 12" between these wires and your power buses. This reduces the chances of electronic noise affecting the DCC signals and makes troubleshooting and access easier.

Once your layout wires are bundled, label them! Many companies offer heat-shrink labels and other fancy products. However, I simply use cable ties having small label tags on them, **25**. You can also cut small rectangles of white styrene, punch a small hole in one end, then slip a cable tie through the hole and attach it to the wire bundle.

My tags are labeled with a code I developed for my wires. For example, B1-NB-MPB tells me the wire is block 1, northbound track, main power bus. For something this complicated it's a good idea to keep a notebook where you can compile detailed notes about each wire run and list the code system for your wires.

©iStock.com/gabes1976

CHAPTER ELEVEN

Basics of soldering

Good solder joints are critical to trouble-free wiring. Investing in a good soldering iron and learning proper techniques will keep wiring problems to a minimum.

Soldering is one of the most important skills you need for wiring your model railroad. Different techniques are required for connecting wires to wires, wires to electrical components, feeder wires to rails and devices, and rails to one another. Let's begin with a look at choosing a soldering iron and accessories, then move on to each kind of job.

Small butane torches with various attachments can be used for soldering, but they can be difficult to control and aren't really designed for small wiring jobs.

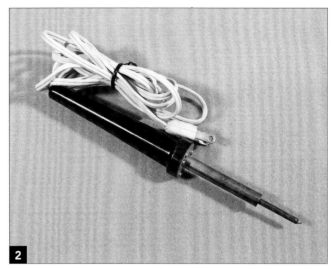

Cheap plug-in soldering irons can be found for only a few dollars, but they typically are underpowered and poorly made.

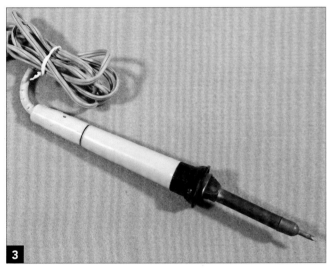

A good-quality iron will last for a long time. I have had this 40-watt flat-tip iron for more than 25 years, and it has served me well.

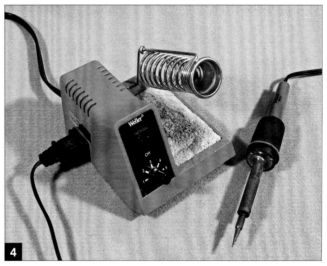

This Weller WLC100 work station is reasonably priced and the iron has replaceable tips. The variable temperature control makes it my go-to iron for almost all my soldering.

Soldering irons

Choosing a soldering iron can seem overwhelming if you look at the large variety of them in catalogs. They range in capacity from under 5 watts to over 100 watts. Skip the small battery-powered irons—I find them practically useless for anything other than very small jobs such as attaching components to circuit boards. For layout wiring you can also avoid butane-powered units, **1**, which put out a lot of heat but can be difficult to control. You can find plug-in models ranging from a few dollars, **2**, to professional work stations that cost hundreds. A nice 25- to 40-watt iron

in the $20-50 range should serve you well for many years. Another piece of advice: If you have one of the old black pistol-shaped soldering "guns," sell it in your next yard sale and get something more flexible and easier to control.

For a number of years I got by with a 20-watt pencil tip and a 40-watt flat tip iron, **3**. A few years ago, after the tip on the 20-watt iron wore out and was no longer available, I upgraded to a Weller WLC100 work station, **4**. This unit can be adjusted from 5 to 40 watts with a continuously variable control. In addition, the soldering iron plugs into the base unit and can be replaced if necessary.

The 40-watt rating produces a maximum temperature of about 900 degrees. The continuously variable control allows excellent temperature control throughout the entire range. A wide range like this is handy because different solder compositions melt at different temperatures. For example, commonly used 60/40 (tin/lead ratio) solder melts at about 370 degrees, whereas lead-free solders melt at lower temperatures and silver-bearing solder melts at over 800 degrees. You also need more heat to solder rail joiners to rail than to solder small-diameter wires to each other. The basic rule is to start with the lowest temperature that will

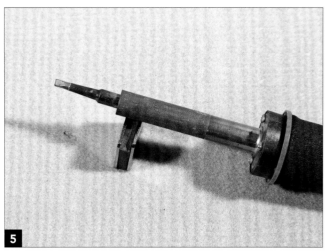

5

To prevent oxidation and increase heat flow, the soldering iron tip should always have a silvery coating of solder on it and look like it is wet.

6

You can purchase individual iron holders—commonly called soldering stands—with built-in sponge pads. Keep the pads damp while using them.

7

I like to use a metal tip cleaner which looks like a brass scrubbing pad.

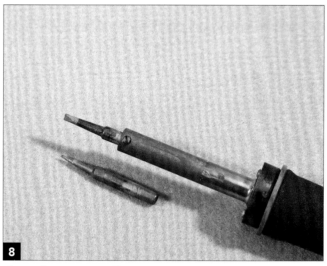

8

The Weller WLC100 offers a number of interchangeable tips. I have found the small pencil tip and the flat screwdriver-type tip to be most useful.

melt the solder being used and increase the temperature as needed to complete the job.

Soldering iron tips are usually copper with a soft iron coating. If the iron becomes oxidized it will be difficult to heat components to be soldered. To prevent oxidation, the tip should always have a coating of solder on it, **5**. Before using a soldering iron it needs to be *tinned*. This is an easy process: Allow the iron to heat up and then apply a light coating of solder to the tip. A little dab of flux will help remove any oxidation on the tip and facilitate the tinning process. Irons should always be stored with solder on the tip. A properly tinned tip is said

to be "wet," and will conduct heat to the work readily. However, too much solder is not desirable and should be wiped off on a wet sponge or tip cleaner before soldering. If a tip gets so dirty that it cannot be wetted, you can clean it with a special polishing bar, but never use sandpaper or a file as they will ruin the tip.

Accessories

There are a number of small tools and accessories that can make soldering a lot easier. The Weller unit comes with a built-in spiral-wound iron holder, and you can purchase individual iron holders commonly called soldering stands, **6**. Another necessary item is

a sponge to clean the tip. Again, the Weller unit has a built-in sponge holder and comes with a sponge. A quick wipe of the iron tip across a wet sponge will remove flux and soldering residues, leaving a silvery-clean tip. I also like to use a metal tip cleaner— this looks like a brass scouring pad, **7**. When you poke the hot tip into the brass curls, excess solder and residues adhere to the brass, leaving a clean tip.

The tip on the Weller iron can be changed quickly using a set screw, providing additional flexibility. I use both a small pencil tip as well as a flat screwdriver-type tip, **8**. The pencil tip is great for soldering electrical components and printed-circuit (PC) boards

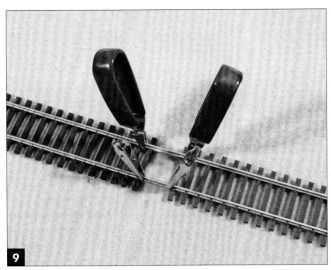

9

These clip-on heat sinks conduct excess heat away from the joint, helping to protect plastic and other delicate components.

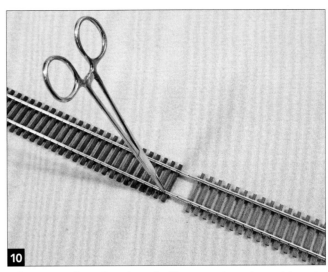

10

A hemostat clipped to the rail will act as a large heat sink and help protect the ties from melting.

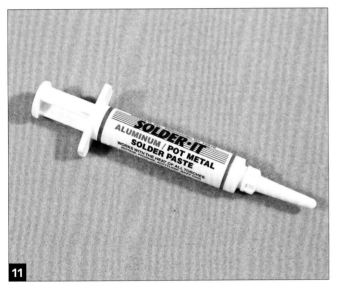

11

Solder-It is a specialty solder that can be used to solder pot metal and aluminum parts.

12

Paste rosin soldering flux can be applied using a small micro-brush. Flux helps clean the parts to be soldered.

since it directs the heat on a small spot, limiting overheating adjacent areas. I use the screwdriver tip to apply a lot of heat to a larger area such as when soldering track feeders and rail joiners to rails. Getting just the right amount of heat is important, since so many things we solder are connected to other things that can melt, burn, or be damaged by excess heat.

To control the excess heat it is a good idea to have some heat sinks on hand. For small jobs, a couple of alligator clips or specially made heat sinks attached to each side of the piece being soldered will conduct excess heat away harmlessly, **9**. For large jobs, such as joining rails, I clip a hemostat or two

to the rails to conduct the heat away, **10**. You can also lay a piece of wet cotton cloth across the rails.

Solder and flux

Solder comes in a large variety of compositions or alloys. The most commonly used alloy for electronic soldering is a 60 percent tin, 40 percent lead composition (written as 60/40), which is what I use for about 99 percent of my model railroad work.

Occasionally I have used solder containing silver (called *silver-bearing solder*) for adding detail parts to brass models. Silver-bearing solder is much harder than the tin/lead alloys, but melts at such a high temperature (over

800 degrees) that it is more difficult to work with. You'll rarely use it for wiring.

Specialty solder is available for soldering what is commonly called *pot metal*, usually a mix of metals largely containing zinc. The one I use is called Solder-It, **11**, and can be difficult to find (check online—it also works with aluminum). Again, it has limited uses in wiring, although I've used it for soldering feeder wires to Atlas turnout frogs. The challenge is that, with the high temperature required, you have to be very careful not to melt the plastic ties and webbing that hold the metal frog in place—this is a good place to use the wet cloth trick.

13

This scratch brush sold by Micro-Mark is great for preparing components for soldering. Replacement brushes are available in fiber glass, brass, and steel.

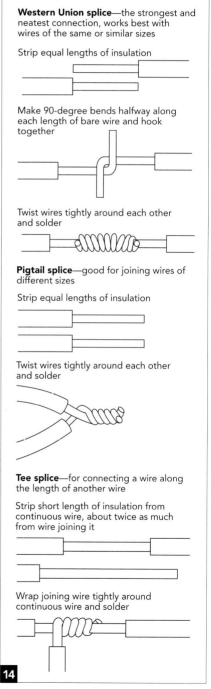

Western Union splice—the strongest and neatest connection, works best with wires of the same or similar sizes

Strip equal lengths of insulation

Make 90-degree bends halfway along each length of bare wire and hook together

Twist wires tightly around each other and solder

Pigtail splice—good for joining wires of different sizes

Strip equal lengths of insulation

Twist wires tightly around each other and solder

Tee splice—for connecting a wire along the length of another wire

Strip short length of insulation from continuous wire, about twice as much from wire joining it

Wrap joining wire tightly around continuous wire and solder

14

These are the most common ways to splice wires by soldering.

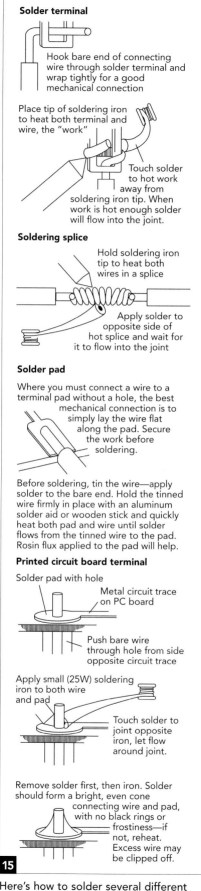

Solder terminal

Hook bare end of connecting wire through solder terminal and wrap tightly for a good mechanical connection

Place tip of soldering iron to heat both terminal and wire, the "work"

Touch solder to hot work away from soldering iron tip. When work is hot enough solder will flow into the joint.

Soldering splice

Hold soldering iron tip to heat both wires in a splice

Apply solder to opposite side of hot splice and wait for it to flow into the joint

Solder pad

Where you must connect a wire to a terminal pad without a hole, the best mechanical connection is to simply lay the wire flat along the pad. Secure the work before soldering.

Before soldering, tin the wire—apply solder to the bare end. Hold the tinned wire firmly in place with an aluminum solder aid or wooden stick and quickly heat both pad and wire until solder flows from the tinned wire to the pad. Rosin flux applied to the pad will help.

Printed circuit board terminal

Solder pad with hole

Metal circuit trace on PC board

Push bare wire through hole from side opposite circuit trace

Apply small (25W) soldering iron to both wire and pad

Touch solder to joint opposite iron, let flow around joint.

Remove solder first, then iron. Solder should form a bright, even cone connecting wire and pad, with no black rings or frostiness—if not, reheat. Excess wire may be clipped off.

15

Here's how to solder several different kinds of connections.

Flux is necessary for getting solid solder joints. When heat is applied to flux, it mixes with oxides and other contaminants on the metal to be soldered, cleaning the metal and helping produce a solid joint. Like solder, flux comes in various compositions dependent on the job to be done. There are two basic types: acid and rosin.

Acid fluxes are very aggressive and difficult to neutralize and remove after use. They are not designed for use with anything electronic or delicate; in other words, they should not be used on model railroads! Acid flux residue is difficult to remove and will continue to eat away at metal components, potentially creating joint failures months or even years in the future. As a word of warning, just about any flux you find at a local big box store will be acidic, even the water soluble ones. The most common ones contain zinc chloride, so if you see that on the label don't use it.

What we need for wiring is rosin flux, typically containing almost pure gum rosin from pine trees. I purchase my flux at Radio Shack, but most electronic suppliers in Appendix B also sell it. Flux is available in both paste and liquid forms. I prefer paste as it stays where I put it. I like to apply it using a small micro-brush, **12**. The residue left from rosin flux can be wiped off using a clean rag or old toothbrush dipped in alcohol.

Many types of solder have flux cores. Make sure you avoid acid-core solder and stick to the rosin-core variety. (I prefer to apply flux directly to the components since I can easily control the placement and amount.)

Soldering step by step

The basic soldering process is very easy and straightforward. First, some warnings—always disconnect any electrical equipment already attached to your rails to prevent inadvertent damage. I also move my decoder-equipped locomotives to another isolated block. Irons are obviously very hot—touching one can result in a potentially nasty burn, so use care, and also avoid contacting paper, cardboard, or other flammable materials.

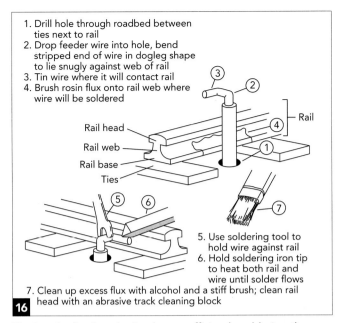

1. Drill hole through roadbed between ties next to rail
2. Drop feeder wire into hole, bend stripped end of wire in dogleg shape to lie snugly against web of rail
3. Tin wire where it will contact rail
4. Brush rosin flux onto rail web where wire will be soldered

Rail head
Rail web
Rail base
Ties
Rail

5. Use soldering tool to hold wire against rail
6. Hold soldering iron tip to heat both rail and wire until solder flows
7. Clean up excess flux with alcohol and a stiff brush; clean rail head with an abrasive track cleaning block

16

Tinning the feeder wire is a key to efficiently soldering the feeder to the rail.

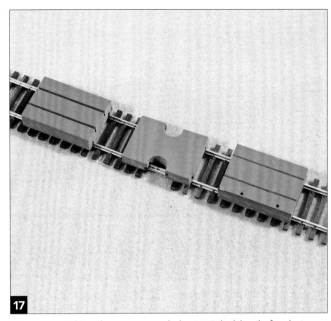

17

These special track gauges made by MLR hold rails firmly in place while hot ties cool so they remain in gauge.

18

Soldering rail joiners (left) provides the best electrical connection at joints, but it's good to leave some joiners unsoldered (right) to allow for expansion and contraction of layout components due to temperature and humidity.

To prepare the pieces to be joined, I clean the surfaces with a scratch brush sold by Micro-Mark, **13**. This brush is available with replaceable fiber glass, brass, or steel-wire bristles. I find steel bristles work best, especially for heavily oxidized material. The brush will leave a clean surface ready to accept solder.

If possible, tin both surfaces to be joined: Apply flux, heat the surface, and melt a little solder onto it. Tinning the components this way reduces the amount of heat it will take to join the pieces later. Next, heat one surface with the iron until the solder on it melts and then put the two pieces to be joined together—sometimes it's convenient

to clamp the two pieces together and apply heat. Apply additional solder over the joint and when it melts remove the iron. Never apply solder directly to the iron, expecting it to flow onto the joint.

Let's talk about some specific soldering jobs, starting with splicing wires. To solder a smaller feeder to a larger power bus wire, begin by stripping about ½" of insulation from each wire and then tin both the bus wire and the end of the feeder. Wrap the feeder wire around the bare bus wire and apply a small amount of flux. Place the hot iron tip on the splice and heat it until solder placed against

the bare wire melts. Allow the solder to flow into the splice and remove the iron. Other types of splice connections, **14**, follow a similar process.

A smooth, shiny surface is a good indicator of a good solder joint. Bad joints, commonly called *cold solder joints*, have a rough, dull surface. Cold joints can be caused by removing the iron before one or both wires are hot enough to melt the solder or by the joint moving as it cools. To fix a cold joint, simply reheat the joint until the solder flows into the wires.

Attaching wires to other components such as terminal strips is a very similar process. Apply the flux and tin

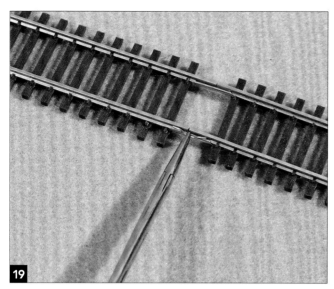

19

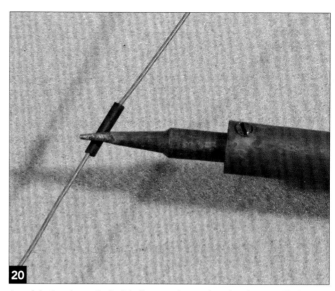

20

To hold a bond wire while soldering, use a hemostat to press the bond wire against the tinned areas of the rail and heat until the joint is complete.

A soldering iron tip held close to heat-shrink tubing will shrink it quickly.

the two surfaces. Wrap the wire around the terminal, **15**, heat the work and apply solder to it. The key is to get both the terminal strip and wire hot enough to melt the solder.

Wiring electrical components and PC boards is a bit trickier. If possible, apply flux and tin the components. This may not be possible with all PCB components since you don't want to obscure a mounting hole or increase the diameter of the component leads. Insert the component lead into the hole, apply flux, heat the parts, and apply solder, **15**. Remember that many electrical components—particularly transistors—are sensitive to heat, so limit the temperature, work quickly, and use a heat sink where possible.

Feeder wires in the 18- to 22-gauge range are commonly used to connect the power bus to the rails. I usually place a feeder on every-other three-foot piece of flextrack. The easiest way to do this is to strip about ½" of insulation from the end of the feeder wire and make a 90-degree bend in the tip about the width of the tip of a pair of needle-nose pliers. Clean the outside of the rail web where you intend to attach the feeder—I use my Micro-Mark wire brush for this. Apply a bit of flux to the rail and tin it. Insert the feeder wire through a hole in the roadbed and tin it, **16**. Place the tinned end of the feeder against the tinned

spot on the rail and heat by placing your iron adjacent to the work. Use heat sinks to prevent the ties from melting. Use alcohol and an abrasive block if you need to clean solder and flux residue from the railhead.

Soldering track joints is easy, but requires more heat and can result in warped or melted ties if you don't use heat sinks. I have some track gauges made by MLR that hold rails firmly in place while things cool so they are kept in gauge, **17**. Clean both rail ends using the wire brush and insert a rail joiner. Apply flux to the rails along each joiner and heat while feeding solder to the space just above the rail joiner, allowing it to flow into the joint.

It's a good idea to leave expansion joints between some sections of track. Whenever you have a joint that uses rail joiners only, make sure each rail involved has its own feeder wire attached to it, **18**.

To bond rails together, bend a piece of solid 22-gauge wire into a "U" shape longer than the rail joiner and tin both ends. Tin the outer sides of the rails just beyond the ends of the rail joiner. Use a hemostat to press the bond wire against the tinned areas of the rail, **19**, and heat until the joint is complete. After a few tries, you'll find that the hemostat will firmly hold the bond wire in place allowing you to use both hands for the iron and solder.

Protecting joints

Once you solder a wire to another one or to a connector, you also need to make sure that it doesn't come into contact with other wires and create a short circuit. Electrical tape is the easiest method, but it can be messy and over time it tends to unravel.

Heat-shrink tubing is usually a better choice. Heat-shrink tubing is a rubbery tube that slips over a splice and is then shrunk down to cover and protect it. It's available in strips and spools in a large range of sizes. The most common types available to hobbyists are PVC and polyolefin.

The PVC heat-shrink tubing I've used tended to melt if touched by a soldering iron whereas the polyolefin doesn't, so I always use polyolefin. The polyolefin shrinks about 50 percent across its diameter when heated, but very little lengthwise.

You can use a special heat-shrink tool or simply use the flat tip of a soldering iron. With an iron you can just hold the tip close to the tubing and it will shrink, **20**. In addition to protecting the joint from short circuits, the tubing also helps prevent the wires from breaking at the joint due to flexing.

One easy-to-overlook key to using heat-shrink tubing: You have to remember to slip it onto one of the wires *before* soldering it!

CHAPTER TWELVE

Signals, detection, and computers

Block occupancy detection—the ability to detect electronically whether a train is in a specific section of track—can be handy for many reasons. It can alert an operator as to whether a hidden staging track is occupied; can automate an accessory such as a crossing signal; can automatically throw a switch in a reverse loop; can activate lineside signals; or can provide feedback to a computer for various train-control purposes.

A Southern freight train rolls past a green signal on Larry's HO layout. There are a number of ways to detect trains and incorporate signals on a model railroad.

1 Magnetic reed switches like this one from Radio Shack are an old method for detecting block occupancy.

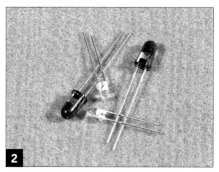

2 Visible-light and infrared emitters and phototransistors are very popular for some types of train detection circuits.

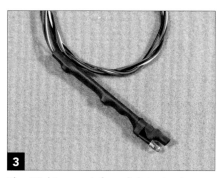

3 The Nightscope infrared detector has an infrared emitter and detector, with an open-collector transistor switch built in.

4 Phototransistors are fairly fast-acting detection sensors yet can easily fit between HO ties.

5 Block occupancy detection sensors like this BD20 have no direct connection to the track bus, instead relying on coils of the track feeder bus wire to induce a sensing current.

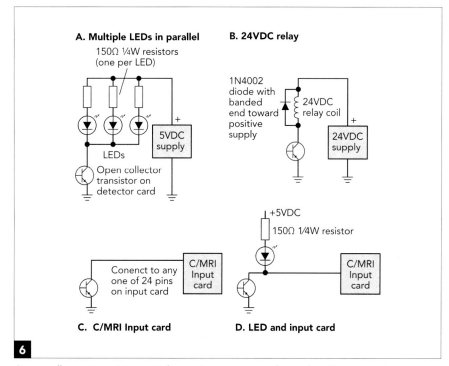

6 Open-collector transistor switch circuits are commonly used as the output to control devices wired to the detector or to switch the logic feed of signal driver circuits.

A number of methods have been used over the years for occupancy detection, including magnetic reed switches, photo sensors, and current-sensing detectors. One thing they all have in common is a connection to an electronic circuit that controls various accessories or connects to a computer interface. Let's start by taking a look at how these detectors work, then move on to some details about each of these functions.

Reed switches

Magnetic reed switches are small electrical switches that contain magnetic contacts, **1**. When a magnet passes over the switch, the magnetic contacts inside move, closing the gap and making or breaking the electrical circuit. They are available as normally open and normally closed SPST switches as well as in other configurations.

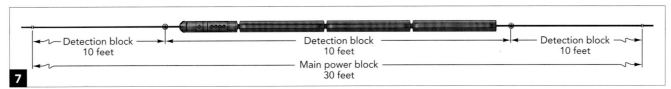

7

Detection block 10 feet — Detection block 10 feet — Detection block 10 feet

Main power block 30 feet

Main power blocks are usually much longer than trains, so several signal-detection blocks will generally fit within a power block.

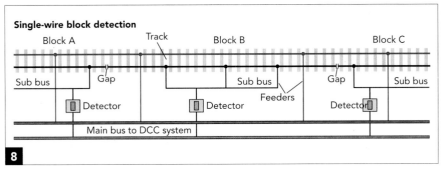

Single-wire block detection

Block A — Track — Block B — Block C

Sub bus — Gap — Sub bus — Gap — Sub bus

Feeders

Detector — Detector — Detector

Main bus to DCC system

8

Detectors are wired into sub-bus feeders within a main block, allowing multiple short detection blocks within the main block.

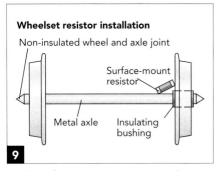

Wheelset resistor installation

Non-insulated wheel and axle joint

Surface-mount resistor

Metal axle — Insulating bushing

9

Small surface-mount resistors can be glued to a wheel axle to provide a resistive load for block detection.

10

Oregon Rail Supply makes these signal kits in various configurations.

12: Resistor values for logic circuit

Input Voltage	R1	R4	R6
5V	150Ω	150Ω	220Ω
12V	470Ω	470Ω	1KΩ
15V	1KΩ	1KΩ	2.2KΩ

The circuit in **11** can be used with varying input voltages by swapping resistors.

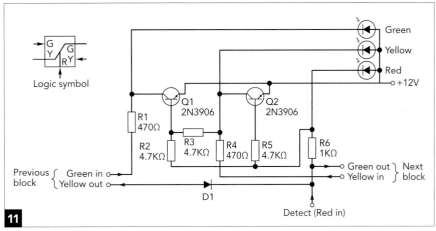

11

Jeff Scherb designed this logic circuit to drive three-aspect signals using the open-collector transistor output from block detectors like the DCCOD or BD20.

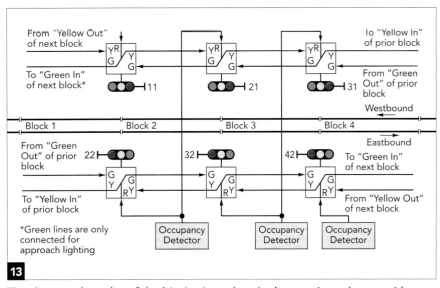

13

This diagram shows how Scherb's circuit can be wired to a main track to provide lineside signal indications in both directions.

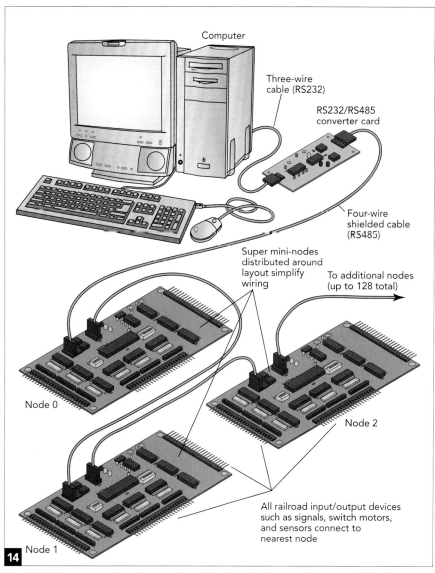

Computer

Three-wire
cable (RS232)

RS232/RS485
converter card

Four-wire
shielded cable
(RS485)

Super mini-nodes
distributed around
layout simplify
wiring

To additional nodes
(up to 128 total)

Node 0

Node 2

Node 1

All railroad input/output devices
such as signals, switch motors,
and sensors connect to
nearest node

14

The C/MRI computer interface works with relatively inexpensive second-hand computers, keeping costs down.

By placing a normally open switch under the rails at a location where you want to detect a train, and gluing a magnet to the underside of a locomotive, the switch will be activated when the locomotive passes over it. For example, if a pair of these is used at a road crossing, you can detect when the locomotive enters and leaves the section protected by the crossing gate and signal. Attach these contacts to the proper electronic circuit and you can turn on a crossing gate and signal.

Reed switches have fallen out of popularity, partially because of the need to attach magnets to the bottoms of locomotives and rolling stock, along with the increasing availability of other more-reliable detectors.

Photo sensors

Photo-sensor circuits typically use photoresistors or phototransistors as sensors to detect the presence of a train. They work based on the concept that as the train passes over the sensor, which is located between the rails, it blocks light from reaching the sensor and triggers the detector circuit, **2**. Photoresistors are slow acting and have generally been replaced by phototransistors in this application. Phototransistors are available in visible- and infrared-light versions, each having drawbacks.

Visible-light photransistors require sufficient overhead light to work properly, and obviously won't work if you run night-time operating sessions

(unless you can install a bright enough streetlight above the sensor). You also might find you need to add more overhead lights if your current layout lighting is too dim.

Infrared (IR) sensors require a source of infrared light to activate the sensor. This can be provided by strategically placing an infrared LED directly over the sensor. Until recently, these were commonly used in staging yards or other hidden places, however a couple products have brought them out of the dark, so to speak. The IRDOT from Heathcote Electronics and the NightScope from Boulder Creek Engineering are IR sensors having both the infrared LED and the phototransistor combined. The NightScope, **3**, in particular has the LED and phototransistor along with the basic detection circuit combined into a single package that can be installed in a hole between the rails. With both devices, the infrared light bounces off the underside of locomotives and cars and is detected by the phototransistor.

Heathcote and Boulder Creek each sell several devices that can be controlled by their detectors. Boulder Creek, for example, produces the WeighStation scale track, TrainBoss defect detector, and the HotShot speedometer.

Photosensors are typically placed either at discrete points or at the beginning and end of the section of track to be monitored, **4**. For this reason they are good choices for detecting trains at single points or in short sections of track (like grade crossings), but they have their limitations when it comes to whole blocks. For example if a switcher is operating at some point in a block between the optical sensors then it will go undetected.

An important feature of photo-sensor detectors is that, because they operate independent of track power, they can be mixed in with other types of detection circuits. For example, your layout might have block occupancy detection for signals using current-sensing detectors, but you could still independently control a grade-crossing flasher with an IR device. On my layout I have optical sensor detectors that control signals at a critical gantlet track. These are installed within a block that uses a current-sensor circuit for the mainline signals in the block.

Current sensors

Current sensors come in two basic designs: diode based and current-sensing transformers. In addition, there are versions that are optically isolated from track power and those that are not—for DCC optically isolated versions are required.

Diode-based units typically have a pair of diodes in line with a track feeder. When there is a load (such as a locomotive) on the track, the track power passing through the diodes produces a current that activates the detection circuit either directly or through an optoisolator that isolates track power from the detection circuitry. The downside to using diodes is that a pair of them decreases track power by about 1.4 volts. Because of this drop in track voltage, current-sensing transformers have become increasingly popular.

Current-sensing transformers work on the principle of inductance. A track feeder is wrapped through the middle of a small transformer coil. When a load is present on the track, a current is induced in the coil of the transformer. The induced current is proportional to the number of times that the track feeder is passed though the transformer coil. This induced current then activates the detector circuit. Because the track feeder only passes through the current-sensing transformer, the track-detection circuit is completely isolated from the track power and thus there's no drop in track power.

Two popular commercial versions of this type of circuit are the BD20 from NCE, **5**, and the DCCOD designed by Bruce Chubb. The BD20 is powered by the induced current while the DCCOD requires a 12VDC power supply. Like most detection circuits, the output of both the DCCOD and the BD20 are open-collector designs, **6**. This means that both use a transistor as a switch that is turned on and off by

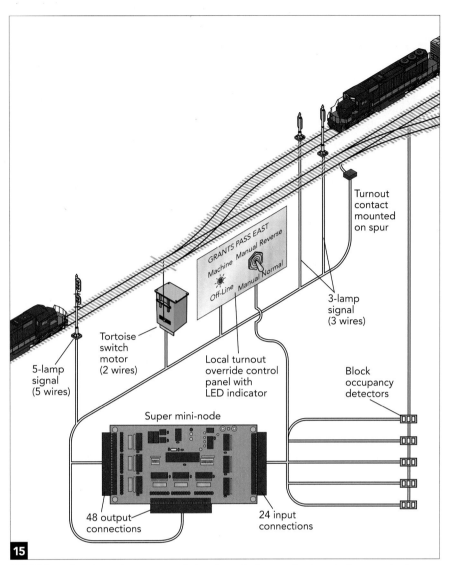

15

C/MRI interface boards can control signals, switches, and other devices on the layout.

the detector circuit. When there is no load present on the track the switch is open; when a load is present the switch is closed, completing the circuit and activating the device wired to it. Most signal systems are designed to work with this type of detector circuit.

Wiring for block occupancy detection and signals

Block occupancy detection (BOD) requires that a layout be divided into electrically isolated blocks. For purposes of signaling, these blocks need to be longer than the longest trains that operate on the layout, **7**. Since main power blocks are usually longer than detection blocks need to be, you may have several detection blocks within each power block, **8**. How does this work? Let's say a main power

block is 30 feet long but your longest trains are only 9 feet. You could easily set up three 10-foot detection blocks within the 30-foot block.

One simplifying factor is that only the track with the detector wired to it needs to be electrically isolated from the other detection blocks. The other rail can be wired as a common rail within the main block; however, you still need to put gaps in both rails between the main power blocks.

When setting up the detection block, don't put a current sensor on every track feeder. Instead, install a sub-bus for all the feeders in that detection block, and then run the sub-bus wire through a single current sensor for that detection block, **8**. On my layout I use 14-gauge solid wire for the main bus and 16-gauge stranded

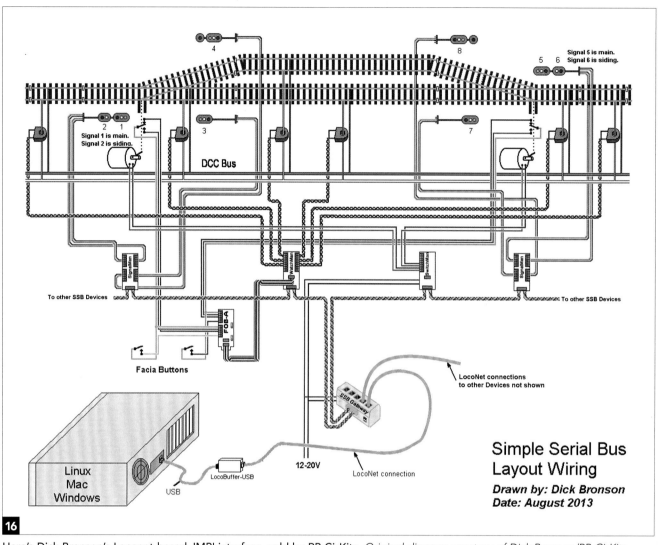

Signal 5 is main.
Signal 6 is siding.

Signal 1 is main.
Signal 2 is siding.

DCC Bus

To other SSB Devices

To other SSB Devices

Facia Buttons

LocoNet connections
to other Devices not shown

SSB Gateway

Simple Serial Bus
Layout Wiring

Drawn by: Dick Bronson
Date: August 2013

12-20V

LocoNet connection

Linux
Mac
Windows

LocoBuffer-USB

USB

16

Here's Dick Bronson's Loconet-based JMRI interface, sold by RR-CirKits. *Original diagram courtesy of Dick Bronson/RR-CirKits*

wire for the detection sub-buses. The smaller stranded wire is more flexible and easier to wrap through the current-sensing transformers.

What is a load?

Current-sensor detectors are turned on when a load is present on the track. In electronic terms, any electrical device that draws current is a load. Locomotives drawing power to operate are the most obvious load for a detection circuit. Even if a locomotive is stopped with just a headlight on, that will usually be enough of a load to trigger the detector.

However, the locomotive is only a small part of the train—and only at one end—so how can we detect the rest of the train? Here's how it works in action: When a train enters a block, the locomotive triggers the detection

circuit as soon as its wheels cross the gap. However, when the locomotive leaves that block, the detector no longer senses the load—even though most of the train is still in that block.

This means adding additional electrical loads to each train in the form of lights or resistors. Lights are an easy way for detectors to sense the continued presence of the train. Lighted passenger cars and cabooses insure that the load required for detection is present. However, if you don't think it looks prototypical to have your trains lit up on a bright sunny day—or if you model modern cabooseless operations—then you can add resistors to your cars.

The most common approach to add resistors to your rolling stock is to wire a 10K- to 15K-ohm resistor between two metal wheels on each car. I've

found soldering is not always a good approach, since it can easily melt any plastic insulating material.

An easier and more popular method is to glue a small surface-mount resistor to the axle with the resistor leaning against the inside of the insulated metal wheel and the axle, **9**. Use a nonconductive glue for this. Once the glue is set, paint the ends of the resistor with conductive paint or glue such as Wire Glue from All Electronics. This creates an electrical path from the back side of the metal wheel through the resistor to the metal axle.

Once the resistor is installed, check the resistance between wheels with an ohmmeter. The meter should show a resistance of 10K or 15K ohms depending on the resistor you used. If your reading is lower than this,

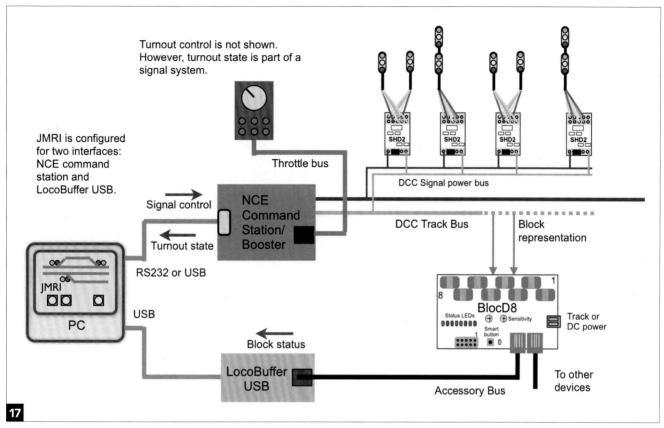

Turnout control is not shown. However, turnout state is part of a signal system.

JMRI is configured for two interfaces: NCE command station and LocoBuffer USB.

Throttle bus

DCC Signal power bus

Signal control

Turnout state

NCE Command Station/ Booster

RS232 or USB

DCC Track Bus

Block representation

JMRI

PC

USB

BlocD8

Status LEDs   Sensitivity

Smart button

Track or DC power

Block status

LocoBuffer USB

Accessory Bus

To other devices

17

Components made by different manufacturers can be combined into an integrated system using the JMRI software. *Original diagram courtesy of Team Digital*

then you probably applied too much conductive glue and shorted across the body of the resistor. If the resistance reading is higher, then you probably didn't apply enough glue to create a good enough circuit.

If the idea of applying conductive glue to tiny resistors doesn't appeal to you, Logic Rail Technologies sells ready-to-install resistive wheelsets. With the BD20 you can also adjust its sensitivity by installing a resistor in slots provided.

So how many of these resistive wheelsets do you need? For reliable detection there should be at least two per car, but do you need them on all your cars? The answer depends on just what you want to achieve in terms of detection and signaling. Some modelers use them on all their cars, while others simply go with a percentage of them and assume that there will always be enough in every train to do the job.

On my layout I have opted to only install detectors on mainline tracks and install resistive wheelsets on unlit cabooses and tail-end passenger cars.

Signals

There are numerous commercial signals and signal systems available from companies like Details West, Model Power, NJ International, Oregon Rail Supply, and Tomar. On my Piedmont Southern layout I have been using Oregon Rail Supply signal kits, **10**. These come in a variety of prototype configurations and are relatively easy to construct.

Once you have settled on which design to use, you will need some kind of signal driver system to control and light them up. Commercial systems are available from Circuitron and others; an internet search will lead you to a number of other kits and circuits. Various circuits have also appeared in *Model Railroader*.

The circuit I use was developed by Jeff Scherb and appeared in the March 2001 MR, **11**. I like this one because it was designed to be used with Bruce Chubb's block detector and is also compatible with the NCE BD-20 and similar detectors. Like most systems, it depends on an open-collector switch

circuit in the detector to activate its logic. With only nine components, it can easily be built on a small piece of perfboard, but the article included a diagram and instructions should you want to make your own PC boards. The logic circuit is designed for three-aspect signals including the block you are about to enter and the block ahead of it. It can operate at 5, 12, or 15 volts DC using different resistors in the logic circuit, **12, 13**. You can get the parts from several suppliers. Space precludes going into detailed information here, but the back issue is available from the MR website (mrmag.com).

Computer systems— C/MRI vs. JMRI

Let's look at using a computer to handle detection and signaling. The Computer/Model Railroad Interface (C/MRI) was originally designed by Bruce Chubb in the mid-1980s. It combines an array of computer hardware with programming to allow users to install prototypical detection

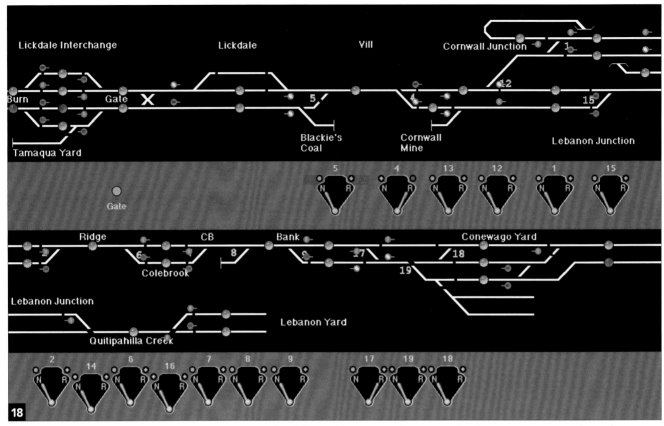

PanelPro, another JMRI software module, gives you the ability to design virtual CTC panels allowing you or your dispatcher to remotely control turnouts and signals all over your layout. *Original diagram courtesy of Nick Kulp*

and signaling systems and automate controls. Chubb's latest series of articles on his updated system appeared in the January through April 2004 issues of *Model Railroader*.

The Java Model Railroad Interface (JMRI) is a system of programs that includes the capability to interface with hardware offered by various manufacturers (including C/MRI hardware) to allow users to install prototypical detection and signaling systems and automate controls. JMRI is a free product that has been developed and constantly upgraded since 1997 by a dedicated group of volunteers, and is well documented and supported.

For a better understanding of the approach used by these systems I have included diagrams from Chubb's January 2004 article, **14**, **15**, and one for the Loconet-based JMRI system developed by Dick Bronson at RR-CirKits, **16**. As you can see there are many similarities in the approaches used, with the big differences being the computer interfaces.

The C/MRI system requires programming by the modeler whereas with JMRI it is basically built into the software. Also, the C/MRI hardware can be used with JMRI software to avoid the programming required, and the folks at JMRI claim that most recent C/MRI installations have actually used JMRI for the computer software. Chubb has information available on his website at www. jlcenterprises.net. More information on Bronson's system is available at www.rr-cirkits.com. Extensive information on JMRI is available at jmri.sourceforge.net, and both systems are supported by active discussion forums on YahooGroups at groups. yahoo.com.

To give you an idea of the flexibility of the JMRI system, I have included a diagram showing Team Digital SHD2 signal decoders and BlockD8 occupancy detectors, combined with a RR-CirKits LocoBuffer computer interface, on a layout being operated with an NCE DCC system, **17**. All these different pieces of hardware are

integrated to implement signaling using the JMRI software.

Signaling in JMRI is implemented in the PanelPro module, which has an especially interesting feature. You can create a virtual Centralized Traffic Control (CTC) panel on your computer that can be used with a mouse or touch-screen monitor allowing your dispatcher, yardmaster, or even operators to throw switches remotely, **18**. This is a powerful feature giving many modelers the potential to create their own CTC control panel—something that previously could only be done for those with enough money, time, and ability to build their own mechanically operated versions. Although you could build a system to control every turnout on your layout, my preference is to only install accessory decoders and BOD's on the main line. This gives your dispatcher the ability to set routes and control signals on the main line using PanelPro while your engineers and yard crews control the other turnouts using switches on local control panels and along the layout fascia.

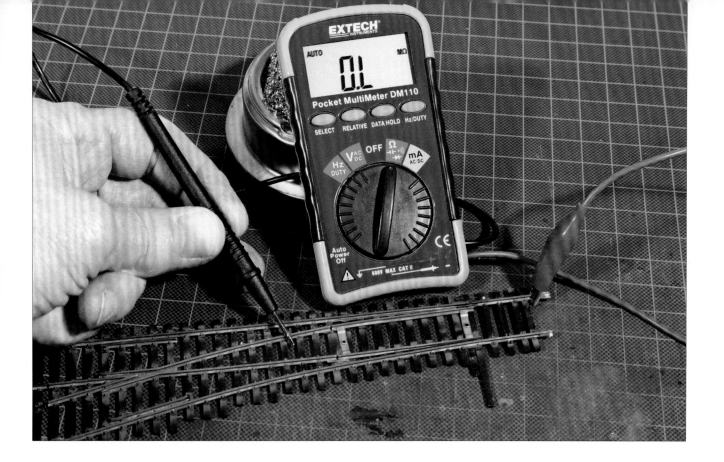

CHAPTER THIRTEEN

Maintenance and accessories

Once your layout is wired, you want to keep it operating smoothly. Problems occasionally surface—a short-circuit won't clear, or perhaps a block mysteriously goes dead—and you'll need to locate the problem and fix it. You'll also need to occasionally upgrade components, add decoders to locomotives, and perform other routine maintenance. Let's start with a look at how a multimeter can assist you.

A multimeter is a basic tool for maintenance and troubleshooting. Moderate to high track resistance values can indicate a bad solder joint, poor crimp, or corrosion, paint, dirt, or grease in a joint or contact. With this meter, a reading of 0.L indicates no connection at the points.

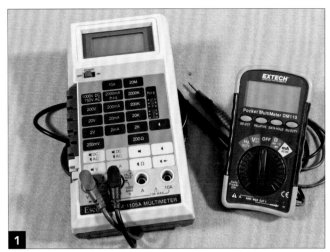

1

The multimeter on the left is 20 years old, yet still performs well. The one on the right is new, is less expensive, and has more capabilities.

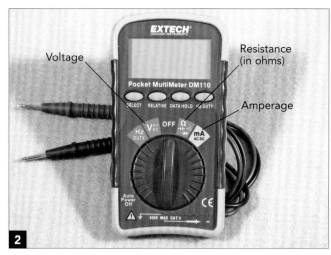

Voltage Resistance (in ohms) Amperage

2

Common handy features include voltage, resistance/continuity, and amperage.

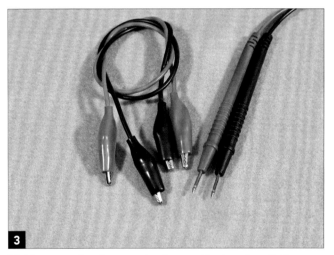

3

Multimeters often have probe tips or alligator clips. Both are handy—probe tips are common on meters without interchangeable leads.

4

A track voltage reading of 4.67VDC with the throttle wide open probably indicates a problem with the power pack or a bad wire connection.

Multimeters

Next to a good soldering iron, a volt-ohm-ammeter—more commonly called a multimeter—is one of the most useful tools you can have for model railroading. Multimeters are available in a variety of sizes, capabilities, and costs depending on your needs and wallet. The vast majority sold today are digital although you can still find analog versions.

As with most tools, you get what you pay for: Don't run out and buy the cheapest one you can find. All the electronic supply houses listed in Appendix B offer reasonably priced meters. Online customer reviews can be a big help when making a selection.

Some features available on high-end multimeters most model railroaders would never use, such as testing a transistor. The common features you'll find useful are voltage, resistance/continuity, and amperage, **2**. Autoranging is a useful feature, but it can add a lot to the cost of a multimeter. The autoranging feature means that the meter automatically detects the magnitude of the measurement and displays it within a meaningful range and in correct units, saving you a bit of mental gymnastics.

Some meters come with multiple sets of interchangeable wire leads. These often have probe tips or alligator clips on the ends—probe tips are common on meters without interchangeable leads, **3**. A set of clip leads work well for connecting probe tips to the rails or other locations. These also are handy for making temporary connections to jump around suspected bad solder joints and dirty switch points, and to test lights and other devices before making a final installation.

One common use of a multimeter is to figure why a locomotive on the track won't run. Voltage measurements allow you to check whether power is on the track, whether power packs or transformers are operating, and whether their output is correct. You can also use the voltmeter function to detect whether there are voltage drops in areas of your layout due to inadequate wiring or other factors.

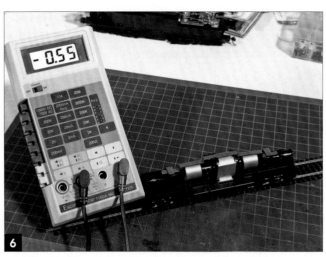

One trick to get a "close enough" voltage reading on a DCC layout is to attach the leads to the + and – wires of a simple bridge rectifier and then place the other two wires from the rectifier across the track.

A high amperage reading for a locomotive may indicate binding in the gears, bearings needing oil, or that the brushes and commutator need cleaning. For this older diesel locomotive a value of .55A at full throttle is about right.

To measure track voltage on a standard DC layout, select the DC voltage setting and place a probe tip or clip on each rail. If your reading is negative, the polarity of the probe tips is reversed—black is negative and red should be positive. Depending on the voltage source being measured, the value may be higher than expected since the output of an unregulated power supply drops once a load is applied. If the voltage reading is zero or lower than expected, **4**, then test the output at the power source. If the source output is correct, then start looking for breaks in the main power bus and wires leading to the tracks.

Always check the most-obvious possible problems on the track first, then the power source, and if all else fails, work backward through the wiring. Start by separating the wires along the current path and measure each section for voltage drops. This is also another situation where blocks can come in handy even with DCC. If you have a switch that can kill power to each block, you can quickly cycle through them and see if the problem exists all over your layout or just in one block.

With DCC, the frequency of the track power is so high that most multimeters are unable to accurately measure it. Remember that the household current most of these meters are designed for is 60Hz, whereas

the DCC signal frequency is much higher—about 6-10KHz. For example, with my DCC track voltage set at 14.5V I get a reading of 83VDC and 15.75VAC. One quick trick is to set the meter for DC volts and attach the leads to the + and – wires of a simple bridge rectifier, **5**. Touch the other two wires of the rectifier to the track and read the value. Using this method my multimeter gives a reading of 14.0VDC. Considering that the bridge rectifier drops voltage by about 1.4V, the corrected value would be about 15.4V—about 1V too high, but in the ballpark and good enough for some quick tests.

For accurate DCC measurements of voltage and amperage I recommend the DCC Specialties RRampmeter, which has special circuitry for the DCC frequency (see Chapter 10 for more on this device).

Amperage measurements are helpful to determine if there are problems with a locomotive that prevent it from running or make it run poorly. Place the locomotive on a test track and wire the multimeter in series between the track and one of the feeders from a power pack. Set the meter for DC amperage and advance the throttle on the power pack. A high amperage reading (say, 1.0A for a new locomotive that should draw .4A) may indicate that there's binding in the gears or mechanism, the bearings

need lubrication, or the brushes and commutator may need cleaning, **6**.

Amperage readings are also useful when debugging a short circuit. Wire the meter in series with one feeder to the tracks. The meter will indicate a very high amperage reading under a full short. This can also happen in a motor itself if excess heat burns through the insulation on the motor wires.

Finding short circuits on a layout can be as difficult as looking for breaks in power buses and feeders. Start by isolating the problem as much as possible: Does the short affect the whole layout, or just a single block? On a cab-control layout, is only one cab affected or both?

Look first for obvious causes like tools left on the rails, metal wheels on a stopped car bridging the gaps at switch points, and locomotives stalled over rail gaps. Examine along the track carefully, especially at turnouts, as it only takes a tiny bit of metal to cause huge problems—a short can be caused by a metal grab iron falling off of a freight car and lodging in switch points.

If you have done recent wiring work, go back and check these connections first. As with voltage problems, check at the track first, then the power source, and finally work your way through the wiring in the area where the problem occurs. Electrical tape may have fallen off a wire, or a stray strand

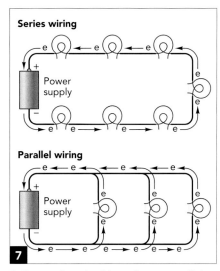

Series wiring

Parallel wiring

7

Bulbs can be wired in series or parallel.

Calculated R2 resistor values for use with LM317 voltage regulator for various voltages

Vout (volts)	R1	R2	Actual
1.5	240	48	51
5	240	720	760
9	240	1488	1.5k
12	240	2064	2.2K

Note: all resistor values are ohms. Actual are the next largest size available.

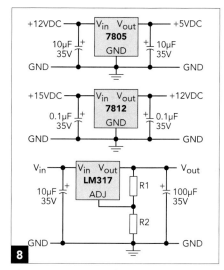

8

The LM317 is a variable-output regulator.

from stranded wire not secured on a screw terminal or not soldered carefully may be bridging a gap at a terminal or electrical switch.

I think I use the resistance setting on my multimeter more than any other. Resistance measurements are useful for debugging many wiring problems. Just set the meter for ohms and attach the meter leads to the wire or track section in question. If there is a good solid connection or solder joint the reading will be zero. Moderate to high resistance values can be an indication of a bad solder joint, bad screw-terminal connection, poor crimp, corrosion, a bad switch, or paint, dirt, or other debris in a joint or contact.

Many meters now have a continuity test setting and will emit an audible buzz as long as there is a resistance-free circuit. By clipping one lead to a rail and then running the other one along the rail and over turnouts you can quickly isolate a high-resistance point.

If you use resistors for various wiring projects, you'll also find it a lot faster to actually measure the resistance of a resistor with a multimeter instead of trying to interpret the color bands on one.

Power supplies and DC accessories

Many layout accessories, from signal systems to structure lights, require a power source in the neighborhood of 12VDC, making an accessory power bus a pretty handy thing to install. Your other option is to invest in several low-amperage power supplies that plug into wall outlets and scatter them around the layout to provide power just where it is needed. The downside to that is that unless you have a dedicated main power circuit for your layout (or you install 120VAC outlets around your layout), you won't have a way to simply shut them all off.

For that reason, I prefer a single centrally located 12VDC power supply feeding a bus. Most electrical supply companies listed in Appendix B sell regulated 12VDC power supplies in a variety of amperage ratings. I strongly suggest this approach, as unregulated power supplies (such as many old power packs) start out with a voltage greater than 12V and can sag below that value under a load.

Select your bus wire size according to the total amperage and length of the bus in order to prevent voltage drops. For long buses I use 12-gauge solid wire. Depending on how clustered your accessories are, you may want to power them with individual feeders spliced into your power bus with suitcase connectors, or run a sub-bus off of the main bus to terminal strips or screw terminals.

For some accessories you will likely need to supply a lower voltage than the 12VDC on your power bus. This is possible using either resistors or voltage regulators.

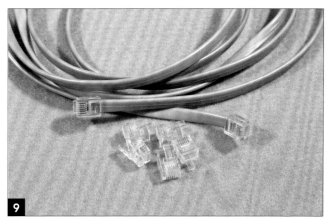

9

Telco cables and connectors are used with DCC command, throttle, and accessory networks.

10

Most DCC throttles have an RJ11/12 connector to connect them to a network adapter.

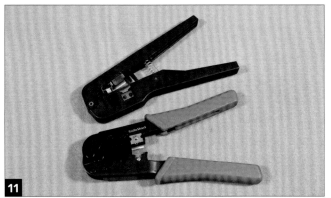

11 These RJ11/12 modular crimping tools are used for cutting and stripping the cable ends and attaching the connectors to cables.

12 Insert the cable end into the cutter and give it a gentle squeeze. The outer sheath should slide off with a gentle tug, leaving the six colored wires exposed.

13 Insert one cable end into the opening in the RJ12 connector. Insert it into the crimper and give it a few good squeezes.

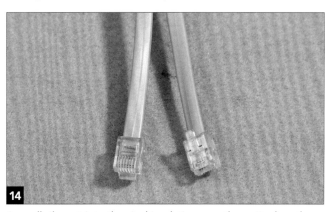

14 A small rib cast into the vinyl insulation runs the entire length of the cable, making it easy to keep track of the proper orientation. Note that the connectors on this cable are reversed.

When it comes to resistors, we have to talk about Ohm's Law. The basic formula is R=e/I where R is the resistance required in ohms, e is the required voltage drop, and I is the amperage of the accessory being powered. Let's say you want to power a 1.5V lamp at 30 milliamps (mA) using the 12VDC supply bus. The calculation would be R=(12-1.5)/0.03 which comes to 350 ohms.

When powering several bulbs, remember that when wired in series voltages are added together; in parallel the amperages are added. Thus to wire three 1.5V bulbs in series you would need 4.5V at 30mA, whereas with parallel wiring you would need 1.5V at 90mA. The problem with series wiring is that when one eventually burns out they all go out, **7**. Of course you could wire a 350-ohm resistor in line with each bulb, but that can lead to a lot of soldering and a lot of resistors. So is there a better solution?

The best way to avoid these problems is to use a voltage regulator. These are small electronic components that maintain a steady output voltage regardless of how many accessories they power. The three most useful for model railroad accessories are the LM7805, LM7812, and LM317. The LM7805 and LM7812 produce 5V and 12V respectively, and the input voltage must be a few volts greater than the desired output. The LM317 is a variable output regulator that can be varied from about 1.5V to over 35VDC by using different resistors. You can see circuit diagrams for each of these voltage regulators in **8**. They also require installing a heat sink on the metal tab to get the maximum amperage. You also need to make sure all attached accessories stay within the rated amperage for each circuit.

Making cables

Chapter 3 explained the various buses used with DCC layouts. Let's take a look at the specifics of how to wire and connect their components. Many, if not most systems, use flat telephone company (Telco) cable and connectors, **9**, to carry the command signal between the command station and boosters. Telco cables are also used to connect throttle plug-in panels, accessory decoders, programming modules, and computer interfaces to the command station. Even throttles themselves typically have a Telco connector on the end of their cables for plugging into the system network, **10**.

Here's how to make a basic system network cable using Telco RJ11/12 cable and connectors. The RJ11/12 cable and components typically have 4 or 6 wires, but since both have six pins, be sure not to mix them up. Since they look the same, what's the difference between an RJ11 and RJ12? The RJ11 connectors have six pins and four wires, while the RJ12 has six pins and six wires. Most systems use RJ12, but

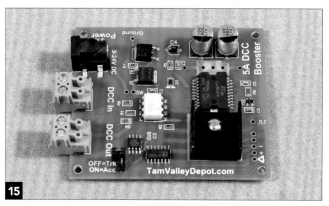

15

This relatively inexpensive booster from Tam Valley Depot is designed for use with accessory power buses.

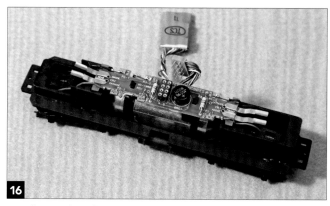

16

Installing a decoder in a locomotive can be as easy as removing the shorting plug in the eight-pin DCC socket and plugging in the new decoder.

17

Several manufacturers also make DCC decoders that are a direct replacement for the light boards in specific model locomotives.

18

To add a decoder to an older Athearn model, start by removing the long metal strip clipped on top of the motor. Many other manufacturers followed the same basic construction.

some are mixed. These components are available in bulk from electronic suppliers listed in Appendix B, and you can also find them at many big-box hardware stores.

You'll need a special RJ11/12 modular crimping tool for cutting and stripping the cable ends and attaching the connectors, **11**. The process is very simple. First, cut the cable to the length you need using the cutting blade in the tool. Make sure both cable ends are square and trim them if necessary.

There's a second cutter or a second position on the cutter that doesn't cut completely through the wires, and has a recess behind it to expose the wires to the required length. Slide each cable end into this cutter and press down—the outer cable should slide right off with a gentle tug, leaving the six colored wires exposed, **12**.

Insert one cable end into the opening in the RJ12 connector, insert it

into the crimper and give it a few good squeezes, **13**. Look through the side of the plastic connector to confirm that the metal pins have pierced the wire insulation. If not, give it a few more squeezes in the crimper.

Now comes the part where you have to do some research. These cables can be wired as straight or reversed. A reversed cable has the same colored wire attached to the same pin at each end of the cable, whereas on a straight cable the color and pin order would be reversed. For example, on the reversed cable, pin 1 might be attached to white wire at each end but on a straight cable pin 1 might be attached to the white wire at one end and the blue wire at the other end. The reversed cable is most common and is technically known as a data cable.

The other big question: How do you know which orientation is correct when working on a very long cable? Most

Telco wire is manufactured with a small rib cast into the vinyl insulation. This rib runs the entire length of the cable, making it easy to keep track, **14**. Recently I have seen cables without the ribbing and in that situation you can tell the proper orientation based on the wire colors at each end. Check your system manual or with your manufacturer's tech support team to find out which type of cable they use.

You can also buy ready-to-use cables, available from some DCC manufacturers as well as many electrical supply companies. I just like the flexibility of being able to make my own cables the exact length I need, since it cuts down on waste and cost. Also, it's likely that a small clip on a plastic throttle connector will eventually break off—being able to replace it quickly by yourself beats having to replace it or ship the whole throttle back to the manufacturer for repair.

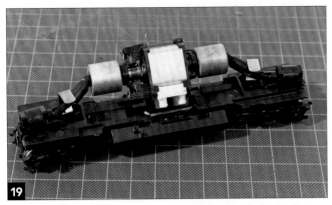

19 Rock the motor while pushing through the four holes in the bottom of the chassis with a screwdriver to remove it.

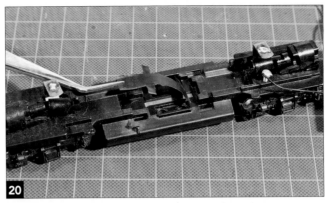

20 Cut a strip of vinyl electrical tape, sized to fit in the area between the motor mount holes, and press it in place.

21 With the motor out of the chassis, flatten or break off the protruding prongs from the bottom bronze clip. Solder the orange and gray wires to each clip.

22 Solder a piece of thin stranded wire between the tops of the two metal uprights on the gear towers.

Accessory decoder bus

Most accessory decoders get both their power and commands from the same booster as the one powering the track in their block. However, this can cause a couple of problems. First, if you have a lot of accessory decoders, they can add a lot of current demand in that block and cut down on the available current for running trains. Second, and more importantly, if a short circuit in a turnout shuts down the booster, you won't have power to your accessory decoder, making it impossible to cycle the turnout and clear the short. For these reasons it can be very useful to have one or more accessory buses just to power your accessory decoders.

Fortunately, there are relatively inexpensive boosters available such as the one made by Tam Valley Depot, **15,** designed specifically for this purpose. These require a 12-18VDC power supply rated at 3-5A and therefore can supply that much current to your bus. Simply feed it the command signals

by connecting it to a track power bus outside of that block and you're protected in case of shorts—plus you'll have more power for your trains.

Installing DCC decoders

Installing a decoder in a locomotive can be as easy as removing the factory installed shorting plug in the eight-pin DCC socket and plugging in the new decoder, **16.** Several manufacturers also make DCC decoders that are direct replacements for the light boards in specific models, **17.** Remove the old one, pop in the new one, and attach the wires to the motor. Some of these require soldering or attaching the headlight wires to the board as well. Many N scale locomotives have circuit boards that can be replaced with a plug-and-play decoder.

The most complex installations involve older locomotives that do not have a DCC socket. Let's go through one of those installations step by step. I'm going to use an HO Athearn

GP60 because it follows an older design used widely by Athearn and others for many years.

Step 1—Once you get the shell off, remove the long metal strip clipped on top of the motor that runs between the two truck towers, **18.**

Step 2—Gently rock the motor while pushing through the four holes in the bottom of the chassis—this will force the vinyl motor mounts to slip out of their holes. Set the motor and its mounts aside, **19.**

Step 3—Cut out an I-shaped strip of vinyl electrical tape sized to fit in the area between the motor-mount holes, **20.** This tape is necessary to prevent the motor from inadvertently shorting out on the chassis later on.

Step 4—At this point you need to decide where the decoder will be mounted. I recommend mounting it inside the top rear of the shell using a piece of double-sided foam tape. This makes the wires for the lights less susceptible to damage when removing

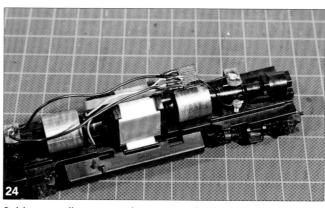

23 Solder the black decoder wire to the top of the screw and the red wire to the top of the rear truck upright.

24 Solder a small connector between each wire and use heat-shrink tubing to protect the solder joints.

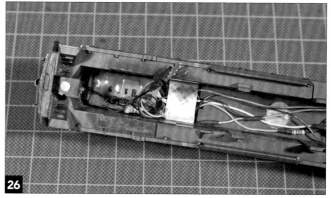

Headlight

25 For models like this I use Miniatronics 1.7mm bulbs glued in place with Testor's Clear Parts Cement.

26 Attach the wiring harness to the decoder and install it permanently to the inside of the locomotive hood using double-sided foam tape.

the shell. Wait until all the wires have been attached before permanently installing the decoder.

Step 5—Turn the motor upside down and remove the bronze clip, noting which end goes under the brushes. Be careful doing this as this clip holds the brush tension spring in place. With the clip removed, note the two prongs bent out from it—either flatten these or break them off.

Next, sand the depression in the underside of the clip and solder the orange or gray wire from your decoder to it. Assuming your locomotive is to be operated cab-end forward, that means the gray wire. Reinstall the clip and remove the top clip. Prepare it and solder the orange wire to it, **21**. I suggest detaching the decoder wire harness from the decoder while soldering.

Step 6—Solder a piece of thin stranded wire (I use 22-gauge) between the tops of the two metal uprights on the gear towers, **22**. These uprights

route power from the right rail. Making a connection to the left rail is more difficult since the Athearn design uses the chassis as part of the circuit path. Drill a no. 50 hole in the chassis behind the motor and insert a 2-56 screw. Solder the black decoder wire to the top of the screw and the red wire to the top of the rear truck upright, **23**.

Step 7—You now should have four wires running between the decoder harness and the chassis/motor. To make it easier to detach the shell in the future for maintenance, I like to cut through the wires and solder a small connector between each wire. Make sure to use heat-shrink tubing to protect the solder joints, **24**.

Step 8—For lights on this model I used Miniatronics 1.7mm, 1.5V, 40mA bulbs. These fit nicely in the headlight openings and can be fixed in place with Testor's Clear Parts Cement, **25**. Wire them in parallel by connecting one lead from each bulb together. This wire combo is then soldered to

the blue common wire on the decoder harness. The other two wires from the individual bulbs are each soldered to a 270-ohm resistor and then to the white wire (front headlight) or yellow wire (rear headlight). Again, use heat-shrink tubing on all solder joints.

Step 9—Finally, attach the harness to the decoder and install it permanently to the inside of the locomotive hood, **26**. You can also use small pieces of double-sided foam tape to pin the wires to the inside of the shell as well. If you used connectors, carefully connect the wires from the decoder to the locomotive and slide the shell on the chassis. Assuming you made no wiring errors, your locomotive should be ready to run.

Cleaning track

Clean rails are very important for getting the best performance out of your locomotives. Remember, anything that interferes with the electrical conductance of the track can result in

27 A track-cleaning block (Bright Boy and other brands) can remove a lot of dirt, paint, glue, and grime.

28 These track-cleaning cars made by Aztec Manufacturing Company are available with various abrasive and cloth rollers that are very effective.

29

This simple cleaning car with a floating hardboard pad, designed by John Allen, has been used by model railroaders for decades.

erratic operation. With DC-powered model railroads this is not nearly as big an issue as it is with DCC. This is because DC locomotives are essentially dumb devices that run as long as there is power supplied to them, and their flywheels provide enough motion to get them over most dirty spots.

However, DCC-powered locomotives have little computers in them, and we all know how computers respond when power is interrupted even briefly. When a DCC locomotive hits a dirty spot on the track and briefly loses power, the decoder inside resets to speed step "0" and the locomotive tries to stop. Once it receives a command update from the DCC system, it will suddenly try to return to the previous speed and the resulting jerkiness can put cars all over the track. If it hits a particularly dirty stretch the locomotive can look like an automobile with a clutch being driven by a first-time driver. Dirty track also

disrupts sound decoders, ruining the effect. These are large enough concerns that several manufacturers have started offering capacitor-based "keep-alive" circuits for their decoders to power them over dirty sections of track.

Fortunately, if you start with clean track and keep it clean you can avoid these problems. The dirt on model track comes from three primary sources: dust in the air settling on it; glue, paint, foam, plaster, and other scenery materials; and oil and grease from our locomotives. The easiest way to prevent dust is to build your model railroad in a finished room in your house. Garages are especially dusty, dirty places for model railroads, and unfinished basements aren't much better. If you must use a dusty location, the easiest way to prevent dust issues is to keep your layout covered with a plastic drop cloth when not in use.

Basements are popular locations, but layouts can receive a lot of dust

filtering down through the floor above and also generated from the cement floor. Therefore, taking the time to finish the basement (at least installing a drop-ceiling and painting the floor) before building the layout is worth the time and investment. If you are a renter or don't plan to stay in your house long enough to justify the investment, then you can limit the problems by painting the floor and using a drop cloth to cover the layout when not in use.

Dust and other water-soluble dirt is fairly easy to remove—simply running a damp cloth over the track will usually do the job. Some scenery debris can also be removed this way, but glue and plaster will usually take some work with a track-cleaning pad or block available from most hobby shops, **27**. Don't use sandpaper or emery boards as they will leave permanent scratches in the tracks and make future cleaning more difficult. The best way to prevent this problem is to cover your rails using

One fast way to remove caked on grime from wheels is scraping it off with a small pen knife. The problem is worse with plastic wheels than with metal wheels.

Both isopropyl alcohol and GooGone work well for cleaning rail. Alcohol residue will evaporate from the track, but you have to wipe off the GooGone with a clean cloth or it will attract more dirt.

To clean locomotive wheels, lay a piece of cloth across the rails and apply alcohol to it. Place one set of wheels on the wet cloth and the other wheels on the track. Turn on the power—the spinning wheels rubbing against the saturated cloth will clean themselves.

low-tack painters' masking tape when doing scenery work.

Once the track is clean, a good way to keep it clean is by adding track-cleaning cars to your rolling stock fleet. I have a couple of commercially available track-cleaning cars made by Aztec with abrasive and cloth-covered rollers, **28**, that can be run in trains or by themselves for special cleaning jobs.

Another option is to make several track-cleaning cars based on the old John Allen design, **29**. These are easy to make using a piece of tempered hardboard cut to fit between trucks. Sand the ends to a 45-degree angle and glue two nails to it. Drill matching holes in the bottom of a boxcar for a loose fit, insert the nails, and the cleaning car is ready to be added to your fleet. As the pad slides along the rails it will scrub them clean. An occasional sanding of the contact

surface will remove the accumulated grunge and renew it for service. I have several of these in my car fleet to keep the rails clean.

Getting the greasy grunge off rails and wheels is the most difficult cleaning problem modelers face. The grease and oil from our locomotives tends to attract and mix with dust and dirt, forming a grey black sticky mess that over time forms a caked-on layer that is hard to remove. It is important to remove this from wheels because if you don't it will rub off them and back onto your freshly cleaned track in no time. Often the easiest and fastest way to remove this caked on layer from wheels is by scraping it off with a knife blade, **30**. The more resistant grunge coating may require an organic solvent such as isopropyl alcohol. GooGone, **31**, is another popular cleaner that can be applied to a rag and then wiped over

the rails—just make sure to follow up with a clean dry rag as any residue left on the rails will attract dust and your grunge layer will quickly reappear.

Several companies make devices for cleaning locomotive wheels but one reliable and cheap method is to lay a piece of thin cotton cloth or paper towel across the rails, saturate it with rubbing alcohol and then hold one set of wheels on the cloth while touching the other set to the rails. As the wheels spin against the saturated cloth it will scrub them clean, **32**. Swap ends and do the other set of wheelsand you're done.

You can also clean rolling stock wheels by simply pushing them back and forth over the cloth by hand. I like to use 91 percent isopropyl alcohol as it is relatively harmless compared to some organic solvents like lacquer thinner.

APPENDICES

Appendix A:
Interlocking panel and signal controls

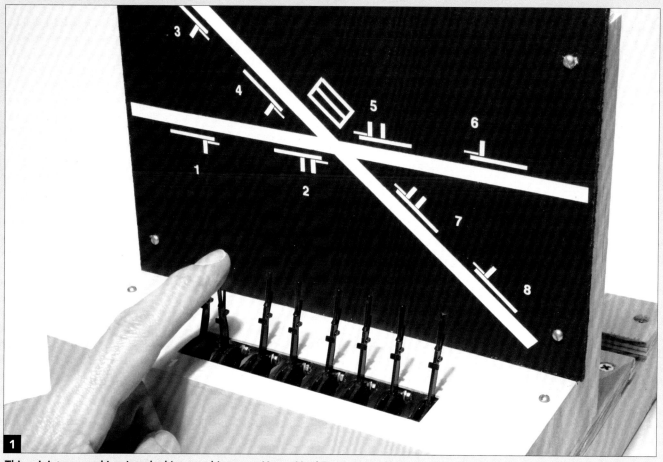

1

This miniature working interlocking machine uses Hump Yard Purveyance levers and a styrene strip locking bed to control signals at a crossing.

The original material in Appendix A was first published in *The Model Railroader's Guide to Junctions,* by Jeff Wilson, published by Kalmbach (out of print). These techniques provide a couple of alternate methods of controlling signals and switch machines.

Wherever real railroads cross or multiple routes meet at junctions, some type of control is needed to keep two trains from trying to occupy the same part of the track. The control system for a junction or crossing is called an interlocking, and consists of all of the signals and turnout controls for that area—all of which are tied together, or interlocked, to prevent conflicting routes from being selected.

Interlockings are fascinating places to model. One option is computerized control, discussed in Chapter 12. However, it's possible—and easier than you might think—to model a fully functional mechanical interlocking, **1**, where several control levers are physically interlocked with each other to control working signals and switch machines. We'll take you through the steps of doing just that.

If you don't want the complexity of a working interlocking, you still can control signals and switches in a realistic manner using Centralized Traffic Control (CTC) style control levers, or you can simply use toggle, slide, or rotary switches.

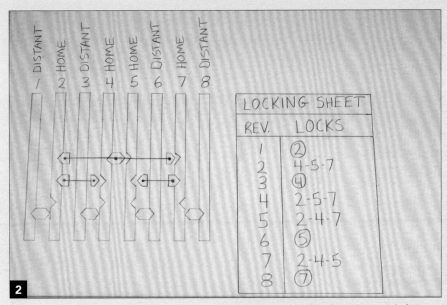

The locking sheet at right lists what each lever must do; the dog chart at left is a pattern for the tappets (vertical bars) and locking bars and dogs (horizontal bars).

The Hump Yard lever kits are molded in engineering plastic, with several types of mounting bases and optional parts included.

Glue the bottom locking bar guide strip in place, making sure it is square to the base.

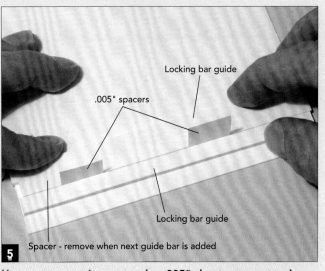

Use a styrene strip spacer plus .005" sheet spacers to place the next locking bar guide strip.

We'll take a look at several available options.

Dog charts

The key to building a working mechanical interlocking is an accurate locking sheet and dog chart. The *locking sheet* is a logic list of what each control lever must do. The *dog chart* shows how the tappets (the numbered bars connected to the control levers) and locking bars with dogs (the bars perpendicular to the tappets) must be arranged to follow the locking sheet.

The locking sheet and dog chart for the simple crossing in **1** are shown in **2**. Each signal, switch, derail, and lock in an interlocking is numbered (although there are only signals in this example). The possible signals are limited, as there's only a crossing and no alternate routes, making this interlocking easy to build. Signals are normally at stop: red for distant signals, and red-over-red (with a permanent lower red) for home signals. Clearing a route will give a green distant signal and green-over-red home signal.

On the locking sheet, the numbers down the left column match these numbered components and corresponding levers. The second column shows the levers that must be locked when the lever in the first column is reversed (a circle around a number means that it must be locked in reverse).

The chart is a series of logic (if x, then y) statements. The control levers at an interlocking must be thrown in a specific order: First is turnouts, then switch locks, home signal, and distant signal. Since there are no turnouts in this plan, the order is simply

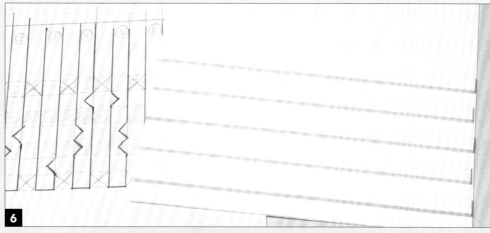

6 All of the locking bar guide strips are shown glued in place.

7 Glue the left-side tappet-bar guide in place, making sure it is perpendicular to the locking-bar guide strips.

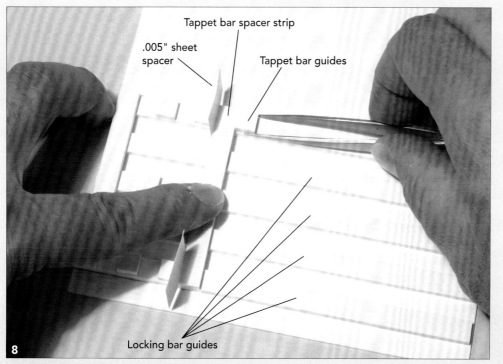

Tappet bar spacer strip

.005" sheet spacer

Tappet bar guides

Locking bar guides

8 Short lengths of .125" x .312" strips serve as tappet bar guides. Make sure they don't hang over the slots between the locking bar guides.

home signal, then distant signal.

For example, for this crossing, clearing (reversing) any of the home signals should lock out all of the other home signals. Thus, on the locking sheet, reversing lever 2 (which sets that home signal to clear) locks levers 4, 5, and 7 (the other three home signals). Reversing lever 1 (which sets that route's corresponding distant signal to clear) then locks lever 2 in position—no other moves are possible unless levers 1 and 2 are moved back to their normal positions.

Applying this to the dog chart, you can see that reversing lever/tappet 2 (pushing it down one bar width) will push the top locking bar out of its notch in lever 2 and into notches in tappets 5 and 7, locking them, and will push the lower locking bar into the notch on tappet 4, locking it.

Let's walk through building an interlocking frame step-by-step, based on the above junction. Doing so will demonstrate how the logic of the locking sheet and dog chart works, and will help you in planning other interlockings.

Building the frame

Once you have established the dog chart, you can begin building the frame. I suggest drawing the pattern for the tappets and locking bars full size. I built my model in similar fashion as Gordy Odegard did in building a working interlocking, which he described in the January through March 1961 issues of *Model Railroader*. (Don Ball built a similar machine, described in the January and February 2015 issues.)

In his original model, Gordy used heavy strip brass for the frame, tappets, and locking bars. This made the model extremely rugged but also quite challenging and time-consuming to build. I used strip styrene to build my locking bed, and although styrene isn't as strong as brass, it has proven to work quite well. A stronger alternative is ABS plastic from Plastruct.

The other key components are the miniature armstrong levers made by Hump Yard Purveyance, **3**. The Hump Yard products are beautiful, large-scale models that resemble prototype levers. The kits also include actuating wire and mounting hardware.

The levers can be mounted in several configurations. I used a flat locking bed and mounted the levers flat in front of the bed, but you can alter this to fit your available space. You can make the panel free-standing, **1**, build it into your layout's fascia, or come up with another mounting scheme.

The levers and locking frame enable you to control signals and turnouts either

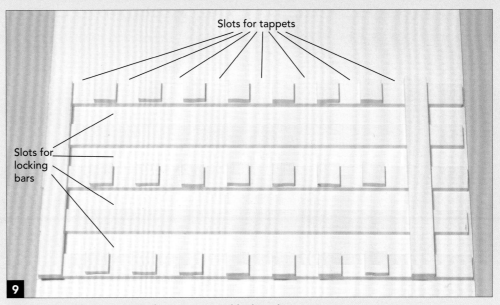

Slots for tappets

Slots for locking bars

9

The finished frame is ready for tappets and locking bars.

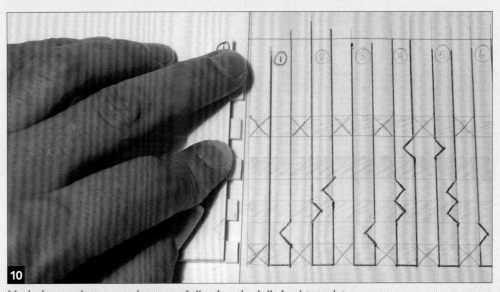

10

Mark the notches on each tappet following the full-sized template.

11

A hobby knife works to cut the notches, but it's difficult to keep the angle of the notch square and the edges of the cut vertical.

12

Micro-Mark's Corner Punch (no. 81652) works well for cutting notches. The inner point of the notch should be at the halfway point of the strip width.

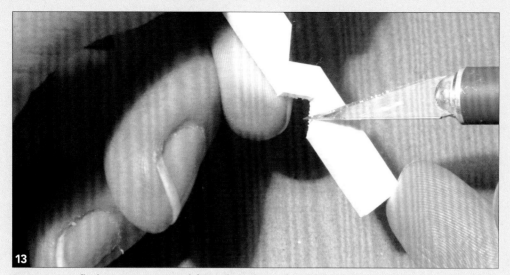

13 Remove any flash or stray material from the edges of each notch.

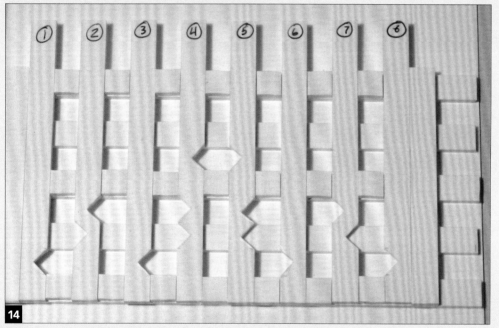

14 The completed tappets are in place in their slots in the frame.

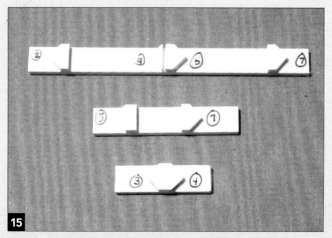

15 Dogs are made by gluing wedge-shaped pieces of styrene on top of the .125" x .312" locking bars. Label each locking bar so you know where it goes in the frame.

16 Cut a pointed end on a styrene strip with a hobby knife or NorthWest Short Line Chopper.

directly by use of actuating wire connected to the tappets, or with electrical slide switches connected to the tappets. More on that later.

Start with a sheet of .040" or heavier styrene for the base. The dimensions should be larger than those of the frame components (I goofed and made mine a bit too short—remember it's easy to trim it later if it's too big). Make sure all edges of the base are cut at 90-degree angles. Use liquid plastic cement to glue the first horizontal locking bar guide piece in place, **4**. These pieces, the locking bars, and the tappets are all .125" x .312" styrene strips (Evergreen no. 390). I found this size to be sturdy enough for the job but still thin enough to cut and work with easily.

The frame must be square to work properly, so check each piece with a square as they're glued in place, **4**. Use a .125" x .312" styrene strip as a spacer in positioning each succeeding guide piece, but with an additional .005" styrene spacer to make sure the locking bar will be able to slide freely in the slot, **5**. As each new guide piece is added, place a styrene strip in the resulting slot and check that it can move freely. Repeat until all of the crosspieces are in place, **6**.

Glue the left-side tappet-bar guide piece (also .125" x .312") into place, **7**, once again making sure that it is square to the horizontal guide pieces. The pieces that guide the intermediate tappet bars are short lengths of .125" x .312" styrene placed on the top, middle, and bottom horizontal guides. Glue these in place, **8**, using another .125" x .312" strip plus a .005" spacer to align them. Use the square to ensure they are perpendicular to the horizontal pieces, **9**.

Tappets and locking bars

Cut eight tappets from .125" x .312" strip to the same length. I cut mine so that in the normal position they're even with the bottom of the lower horizontal guide and ¾" above the top guide (where they will meet the levers). Set them in place and make sure they move freely in their slots. Use a permanent marker to label them with their numbers.

Starting with tappet no. 1, follow the full-size template and dog chart and mark the lever where it is to be cut by setting it in place atop the frame. Make sure its bottom is even with the edge of the bottom locking bar guide strip, **10**. Use a pencil to mark the tappet. The top and bottom of each notch should align with its corresponding horizontal locking bar slot.

You can use a chisel-tip hobby knife to cut the

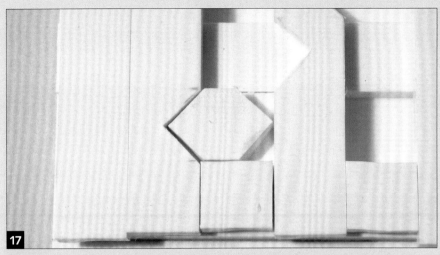

17

The completed dog or dogs should have a minimal amount of play. Test each as they're built.

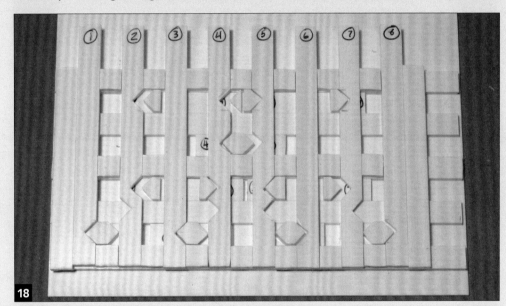

18

All locking bars are in place and tappets are in their normal positions, ready for testing.

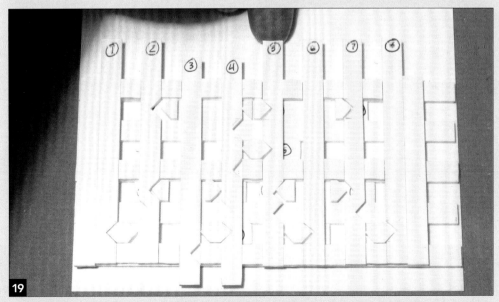

19

With tappets 3 and 4 reversed, tappet 5 can't move—the dogs are properly locking out all other tappets.

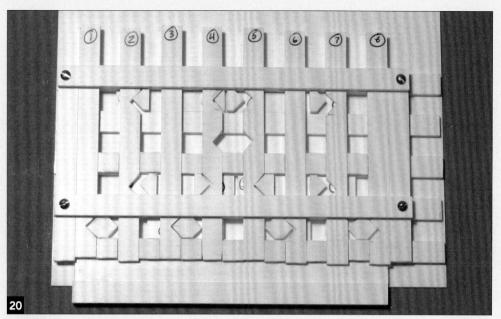

20 Use screws to secure a pair of strips across the tappets to hold them in place. Glue a strip across the bottom to act as a stop for the tappets in the reversed position.

respective notches. Make sure that all of the tappets and locking bars operate smoothly before moving to the next steps.

During testing, I discovered that the second locking bar from the top was unnecessary (which is reflected in the dog chart in **2**. Note that later photos have this locking bar removed.

Once the parts are working properly, add two styrene strips across the tappets to hold them in position, **20**. Place them over the top horizontal locking-bar guide and the next-to-bottom guide, since you'll need access to the bottoms of the tappets. Secure these with 2-56 screws. Don't glue them— the tappets or locking bars might need later fixing or adjusting.

Also add a bottom strip as a stop for the tappets. This should be one strip width (.312") from the bottom of the tappets' normal position. This provides a positive stop for the tappets at a width of one locking bar. Here's where I wish I would have made the base for the frame a bit longer—I had to add a small piece as an extension for the stop.

notches, **11**, but a Micro-Mark corner cutter (item no. 81652) will be much faster, **12**. The corner cutter can be mounted in a drill press (not turning). Pulling down on the press handle cuts the notch. The result is a perfect 90-degree cut every time.

Use a hobby knife to clean any flash or jagged edges from the notch, **13**, then place the tappet back in the frame to make sure it moves freely in its slot. The completed tappets in place in the frame are shown in **14**.

Let's move to the dogs. You can see a few completed dogs in **15**. Cut

a 90-degree pointed end on a .125" x .312" strip, **16**, trim the end from the strip, and glue it on top of a .125" x .312" styrene strip locking bar.

The dimensions of the dogs are critical to the function of the locking bed. Use the tappets as your measuring guide, and test each dog and locking bar as they're completed to make sure they fit properly. They shouldn't fit snugly—leave just a bit of play, but not much more than 1/32" or the lever will be able to move too much. You can see the proper fit of the small dog

between tappets 1 and 2 in **17**.

Photo **18** shows all of the tappets and locking bars in place, with the tappets in their normal positions. Now's the time to play with the locking bed, both to get a feel for how the system works and to make sure the levers lock each other out as they should.

Test all possible lever combinations. In **19** you can see that tappets 3 and 4 are reversed, and it shows that tappet no. 5 (and all other tappets) can't be moved. All of the dogs are doing their jobs, locking into their

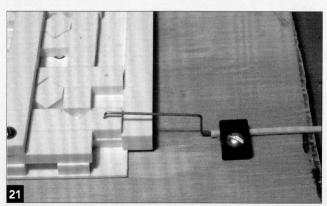

21 Actuating wire can be added to the ends of the tappets to control turnouts and signals directly.

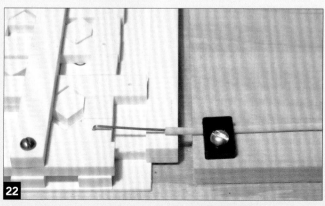

22 Mounting the actuating wire guide on a wood base eliminates the need to bend the actuating wire.

23

Slide switches can be mounted in holes or a gap in the plywood at the end of the frame. Each switch must line up with its tappet.

24

With tappet and switch reversed, mark the connecting strip at the left of the screw shaft to indicate the amount of throw needed.

25

Move the tappet and switch to the normal positions, then mark the strip to the right of the screw head.

26

The connecting strip throws the slide switch as the tappet moves between normal and reversed positions.

Signals and turnout controls

You can use the motion from the tappets to control signals and turnouts in several ways. We'll look at a couple of them. No doubt you can come up with other methods as well.

Start by securing the locking bed to a piece of plywood. My locking frame measures about 5½" wide by 4¼" long, and its styrene base is 6" square. The size of the wood base will depend on how you will mount the frame to your layout.

You can use actuating wire to control turnouts and semaphore signals directly.

The Hump Yard levers include a length of actuating wire that's encased in a plastic sleeve, and it works very well for the job. You can see one way to connect this wire to the end of the tappets in **21**. Drill a hole the appropriate size in the end of the tappet to accept the wire, and clamp the wire guide near the end of the tappet.

Another option is shown in **22**, elevating the actuating wire connection to avoid the wire bends needed in the earlier installation.

You also can use the tappets to control electrical slide switches, which then can be used to power turnouts or signals. I mounted the switches by mounting two pieces of plywood with a gap between them on a 1 x 2 frame, **23**. The switches sit in this gap and are nailed or screwed in place, aligned with the tappets.

The throw distance on the tappets matches the distance between the locking bars (.312"), which is longer than the throw on the DPDT microswitches that I used (Miniatronics no. 38-200-05). This will vary for you depending on the switches you use,

but adjusting for this isn't difficult.

Use thin styrene or ABS strips (I cut .250"-wide strips from a scrap .040" styrene sheet) to transfer the motion from the tappets to the switches. Drill a no. 50 hole in the end of the tappet and tap it for a 2-56 screw; do the same in the top of each slide switch. Drill a no. 42 hole in one end of the connecting strip to clear the screw on the tappet end.

Start with tappet no. 1. Set the tappet in the reversed position and throw the slide switch away from the tappet. Place the connecting strip in the

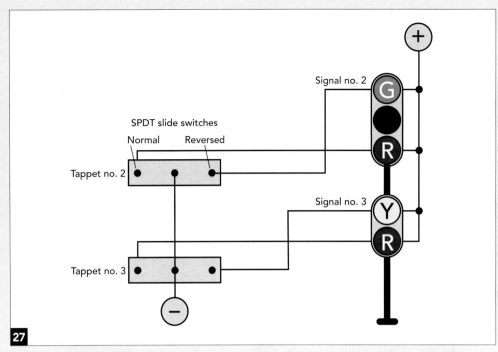

27

Here's one way of using slide switches to control signals. You can adapt them to various situations (such as having separate home and distant signals).

28

Drill mounting holes for the Hump Yard levers following the template in the instructions.

by mounting the control levers in place. Many different approaches can be taken for assembling and mounting the Hump Yard levers (most of which are detailed in the product's instructions). You can mount the panel and locking bed vertically to save space, or you can do as I did and mount it flat. Once again, be creative and play with the various components.

Mounting on a flat surface requires the bottom of the lever to be trimmed and a new mounting hole drilled for the wire connector. The instructions include a template for drilling mounting holes. Drill these so each lever will be aligned with its tappet, **28**.

You'll need to connect the bottom of each lever to its tappet. I used .025" wire from the Hump Yard actuating wire. This wire must be heavy enough not to twist when moved. The amount of throw from a hole drilled at the bottom of the lever was just about perfect for the .312" width of the locking levers. You may have to adjust the shape of the wire depending upon your installation, **29**.

Test the lever with the wire to make sure it works properly. The lever must push the tappet all the way to the bumping strip when the lever is thrown. You can see two levers and wires installed in **30**. Cutting a gap in the spacer on the tappet side of the lever mounting base allows the wire to pass between the lever's mounting legs to the tappet.

As you design and build your machine, keep in mind that the arrangement of the levers and tappets from

proper place on the tappet, **24**, and mark the strip at the left edge of the screw shaft. This indicates the amount of throw needed. Next, move the tappet to the normal position and throw the slide switch toward the tappet. Mark the strip at the right edge of the screw shaft, **25**. This indicates how much motion is needed to pull the slide switch back toward the tappet.

Use these marks as a guide for cutting a notch in the connecting strip. Remove the screw from the switch, place the connecting strip in place, then attach it by adding the screws at each end, **26**.

You can use the slide switches to control signals directly, **27**. To control turnouts, follow wiring instructions for the make of switch machine you're using.

You also can combine mechanical and electrical control by connecting an actuating wire to the end of the connecting strip. For example, you can use the slide switch to control indicator lights on a control panel while using the actuating rod to mechanically throw a semaphore.

Connecting the levers

You now can place the whole machine in business

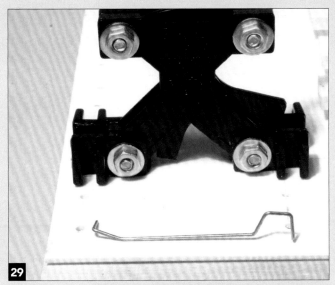

29

The bottom of the lever has been trimmed, and a new hole drilled for the wire. Shape the wire to match the tappet and lever.

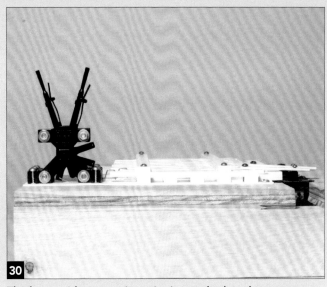

30

The lever with connecting wire is attached to the tappet.

left to right will depend on the end of the tappets where the levers are located. I originally had planned to have the levers to the rear of the locking bed, but it worked best for my installation to have the levers in front of the locking bed, **31**. This requires the tappets to be located in a mirror image compared to the original dog chart (or else your levers will be numbered from 8 to 1 from left to right).

This wasn't critical for this particular interlocking because it is symmetrical (levers 1 and 8 are mirror images of each other, as are 2 and 7, etc.). Thus, on my model, lever 8 became lever 1 and so on. Keep this in mind as you design and build your own machine.

Frame and track diagram

I covered the frame bed, **31**, while allowing the levers to come through a fake floor. The L-shaped side brackets are cut from ½" plywood. The dimensions aren't critical, and will vary

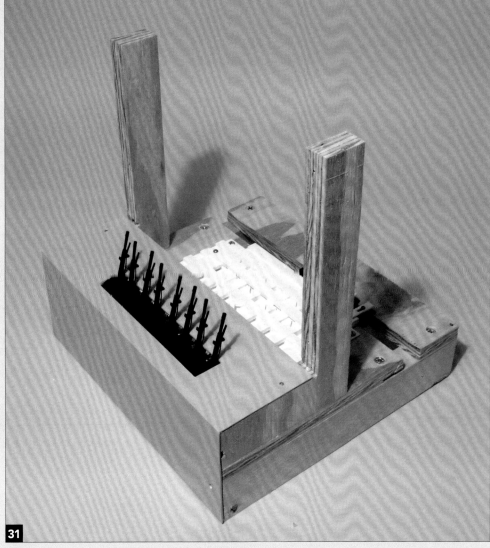

31

The frame is made of plywood. The L-shaped cover over the levers is sheet styrene, screwed in place to allow later access if needed for maintenance.

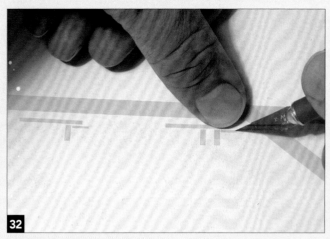

Use strips of thin masking tape to mark track and signal locations.

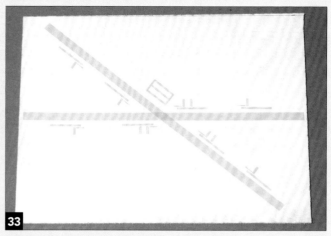

The masking tape is applied, and the board is ready for black paint.

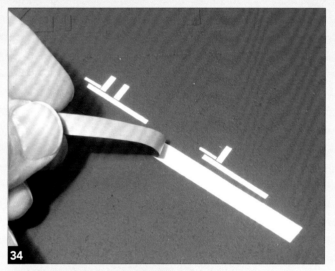

Peel the masking tape away to reveal the track diagram. Touch up any areas as needed with a brush.

Dry transfers work well for marking signal numbers and any other lettering needed.

depending upon your available space. The front and top surfaces are .040" styrene, cut to fit, with a slot cut in the top to allow the levers to pass through. The styrene pieces are glued together to form an angle, and the completed piece is screwed to the frame to allow access to the mechanism.

The track diagram, also screwed in place on the frame, is essential to let operators know which levers correspond with each turnout and signal. These can be made in several different ways. I used the tried-and-true masking-tape-

and-paint method, which has been popular for years in building control panels.

Thin (⅛") tempered hardboard, such as Masonite brand, works well for these, and heavy styrene will also work well. The overall size of the diagram can vary depending on the complexity of the diagram and how you choose to mount it. Start by painting the board white. Use strips of ¼" masking tape to mark the track location on the board. Next, use tape to mark the signal locations, **32**. This looks complex at first, but the process is simple and goes quickly.

I laid a strip of ¼"-wide masking tape on a piece of glass, then cut it in both thick and thin segments to represent semaphore blades. The thick pieces mark the blades at their normal aspects, while the thin pieces show the blade position when reversed. Use more pieces of narrow (.080") tape to mark the outline of the interlocking tower location on the diagram. Photo **33** shows the masking in place. Make sure the tape is burnished firmly to the board so no paint leaks under it.

Paint the board a contrasting color. I used a

spray can of flat black paint. Use light coats, making sure the board is completely covered. Once the paint is dry, peel the masking tape off, **34**, and touch up any areas as needed.

Add numbers to the signals and turnouts using dry transfers, **35**. I used a lettering set from Woodland Scenics. Burnish the transfers firmly to the board, then remove the backing sheet.

As **1** shows, my board simply shows the track layout and numbers, but you can easily dress up your board by adding indicator lights to show the position of signals and turnouts or to show track occupancy. Mount the track plan to the frame, and your interlocking machine is complete.

You can use other methods to make track diagrams, including designing and printing them from a computer as discussed in Chapter 9. This works well if you have a lot of lettering, artwork, and logos to include. You can also use colored pinstriping tape on backgrounds of various colors.

Designing dog charts

You can use the above methods to build other simple or complex interlocking machines. Here are a couple of other samples to get you going.

Figure **36** shows a simple junction with a branch line diverging from a main line, together with the dog chart for the junction. This interlocking has a single turnout and three possible routes. The three home signals are normally red-over-red, and the distant signals are normally at yellow. The home signals for trains entering at A and B have permanent lower red signals because only one route is possible. Lining the route for trains entering at A results in green-over-red (clear), while lining the route for trains entering at B gives a yellow-over-red (approach) aspect because it's a slow speed route.

For trains coming from C, lining the straight (normal) route to A provides green-over-red, while lining the slower speed route to B gives a red-over-yellow (diverging approach) aspect. You can change these aspects to match the desired

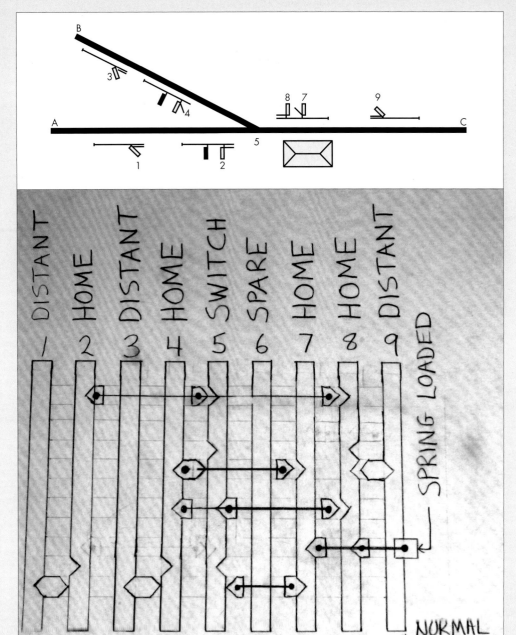

36

Here's a simple diverging (non-crossing) junction with its dog chart.

speeds for your modeled routes.

The dog chart isn't much more complex than the earlier crossing, but it does include a spring-loaded locking bar. Gordy Odegard's brass locking bed provides an example, **37**.

You can see the track plan for Gordy's original machine, with the dog chart, in **38**.

You can apply these

charts and ideas to similar and more complex junctions. Start by writing a locking chart for all signals and switches, then carry the pattern to the dog chart. In designing and building your own locking bed, you're bound to end up with a notch or two in the wrong place. Try to work through it, and keep playing with the lever combinations until the machine works properly.

CTC-style board

With the growing popularity of all-relay interlocking systems in the 1930s and 1940s, many junctions became controlled by panels of a similar style to Centralized Traffic Control dispatcher's panels. Boards such as the one in **39** are easy to build thanks to the nice plates and knobs offered by Rix Products (kit no. 628-61, **40**). These

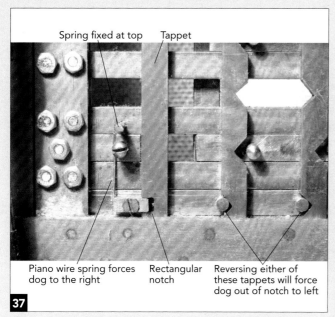

Spring fixed at top   Tappet

Piano wire spring forces dog to the right

Rectangular notch

Reversing either of these tappets will force dog out of notch to left

37

Some locking beds require spring-loaded locking bars.

are molded in silver plastic and must be painted. The best way to do this is to paint them semi-gloss black (I used a spray can), then rub their faces on fine sandpaper. This neatly removes the paint from the raised letters and details as seen in **40**. Rix provides decals to use for numbering the plates.

Building a working interlocking is more complex with these components compared to the lever/mechanical plant. We'll look at controlling a junction, but without the actual interlocking mechanism.

Many model railroaders have used computers to control interlockings of this type—see Chapter 12 for some guidelines.

Start by planning your control panel. Its size will be determined by your available space and location as well as by the complexity of the trackwork and number of control switches needed.

As with the mechanical interlocking, you'll need to determine the number of signals, their locations, and the aspects desired. I followed the same basic plan as in **36**, but with a permanent yellow approach signal on the branch and approach signals on the main line that usually are at yellow and go to green when reversed, **41**.

With this type of machine, turnouts are given odd numbers and signals even numbers. Both are numbered from left to right. The turnout panel switches are in the top row; the bottom row is for signal switches.

For turnout switches, the N and R indicate normal and reversed positions (with corresponding red indicator lamps). The normal route of a turnout generally is shown on the track diagram with an unbroken line (straight on our model), with the reversed position indicated by a break in the line.

For the signal switches, L and R indicate that signals are cleared to the Left or Right, with corresponding green indicator lamps; when positioned in the middle, the red middle lamp is lit. Note that signals on the diagram are numbered with an L or R, indicating the direction of travel they govern.

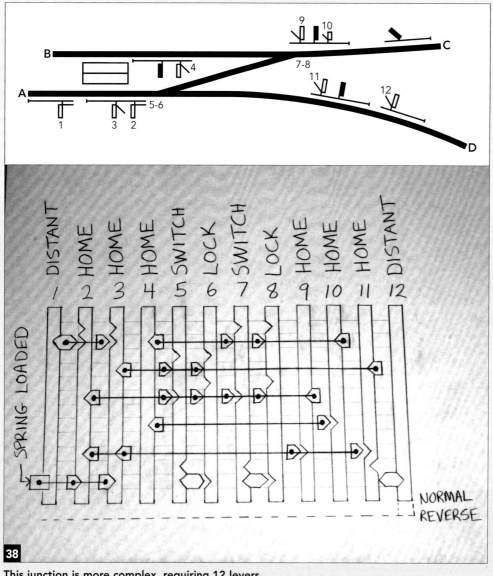

38

This junction is more complex, requiring 12 levers.

Our model is simplified compared to the real thing. For example, a real panel would have a code button below the control switches that would actuate the switch settings. You can use one switch for each signal head; doing so makes the wiring easier but will also require more components and therefore more space on your fascia or control panel.

It's best if you can do as the prototype does: control two opposing signals with a common rotary switch, with the L and R indicating the route is cleared for travel toward the left or right per the track diagram. For example, on our sample the signal 4 switch aligns the opposing home signals for the straight route, and the signal 6 switch aligns the opposing home signals for the diverging route.

As the photos show, if a control switch sets a signal for one direction only (as with distant signals 2R and 8L), then only one directional indicator lamp is needed.

Building the panel

Figure 42 shows the full-sized template I made on a pad of drawing paper for marking the center points of the mounting holes for the rotary switches and panel indicator lights. The dimensions I used for spacing switches next to each other are shown in 43. I used tempered hardboard for my panel; you can also use thin plywood or other thin material.

Tape the template in place over the panel, then transfer the markings to the board by poking through the template with an awl or scriber.

39 Panel switches from Rix make it easy to build panels based on all-relay interlocking machines.

40 The Rix plates are molded in silver plastic (left). Painting them black (middle) and then sanding the letters and trim gives a realistic appearance.

Drill mounting holes for each component. Your hole dimensions will depend upon the shaft size of your rotary switches (⅜" is common) and lamps (I used bulbs from Radio Shack that required ½" holes). A spade bit works best for drilling hardboard, as its design will cut the material cleanly without pulling material out, as a regular spiral bit tends to do.

Prototype panels had small knockout disks covering unused holes. To simulate these, add disks of ½"-diameter, .020"

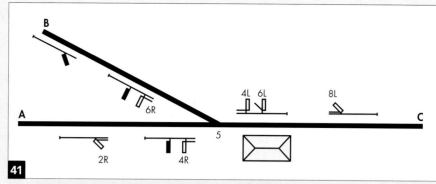

41 Here's the signal labeling for the junction panel in **39**.

44 The Rix knob fits nicely over the D-shaped knob of the rotary switch.

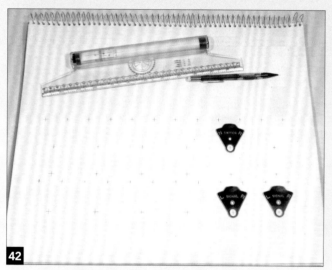

42 Draw a full-sized template for your control panel.

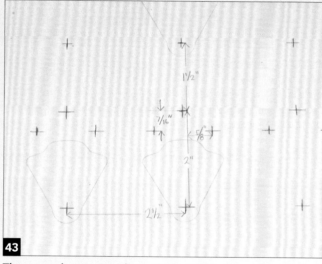

43 These are the spacing dimensions used for the components.

styrene to the unused switch and lamp positions. Use cyanoacrylate (CA) to glue them in place.

Assembly

I used the same masking tape technique as with the board in **1**. I painted my panel dark green—a common color for these panels—using a spray can.

The indicator lamps are ½"-mount, 12-volt bulbs from Radio Shack (nos. 272-332 red, 272-337A green). They work perfectly for these panels and would work for many other projects as well. Simply push them into place on the panel; the sprung side clips on their housings will hold them in place.

I used CA to glue the Rix switch plates in position,

although the rotary switches will hold them securely once they're installed. The photos show a two-pole, six-position rotary switch with a ⅜" mount and D-shaped shaft, **44**.

A 2P6T (two-pole, six-throw) rotary will control the signals, but to get the indicator lamps operating off the same switch you'll need a rotary with two layers (or wafers), **45**. Use non-shorting rotary switches with 30-degree spacing contacts.

Wiring will depend on the signals you're using. If you're using a type of color light signals with LEDs or bulbs, follow the diagram in **45**. That diagram shows how signal switch 4 and signals 4R and 4L are wired. The voltage used will depend on

the type of LED or bulb you're using. Note that polarity must be correct when using LEDs, and you'll need to use appropriate resistors—see Chapter 13.

You can modify the circuits to control switch machines, signal drivers, and other accessories. You also can simplify any of the above controls and simply use slide, toggle, or rotary switches to control turnouts and signals. Figure **46** shows some simplified control circuits, and the following section shows how to actuate a semaphore with a slow-motion switch machine.

Semaphore control

For realistic operation, semaphore blades should move slowly. The following

instructions from Jeff Scherb show how it can be done. A slow-motion switch motor can provide the animation, but these switch motors generally only have two positions, and this type of semaphore needs three. Fortunately, Circuitron's Tortoise switch motor can easily be wired to have the needed third (center) position.

Circuitron produces a remote signal-actuator mounting bracket and vertical motion mechanism that adapts Tortoise switch machines to operate semaphore signals, but it's not hard to make your own drive mechanism—here's how Jeff did it, **47**.

An actuating lever is made from .025" x ¼"

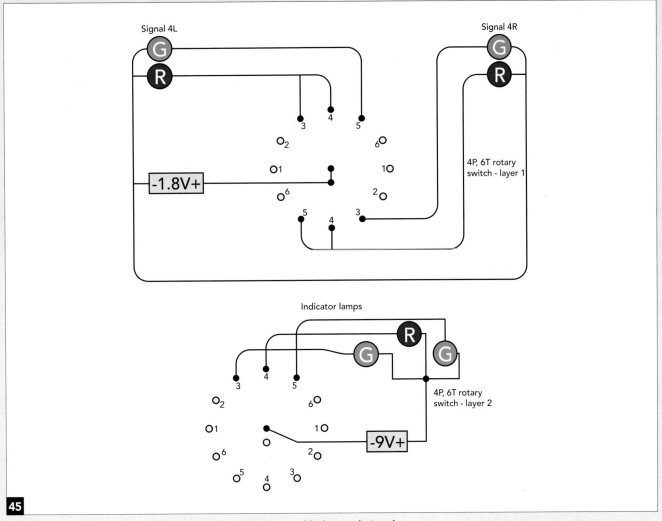

45

A 2P6T rotary switch with two wafers controls both panel lights and signals.

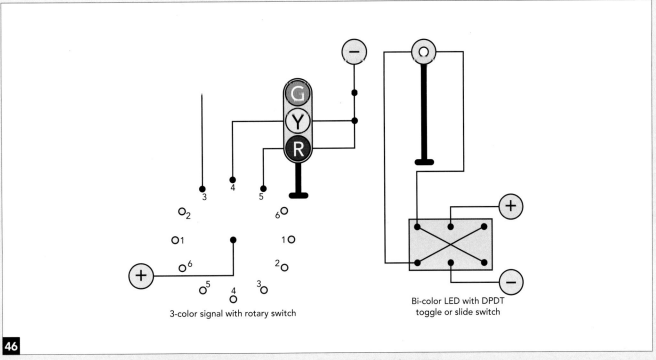

46

Here's another way of controlling a three-light signal or a signal with a bi-color LED.

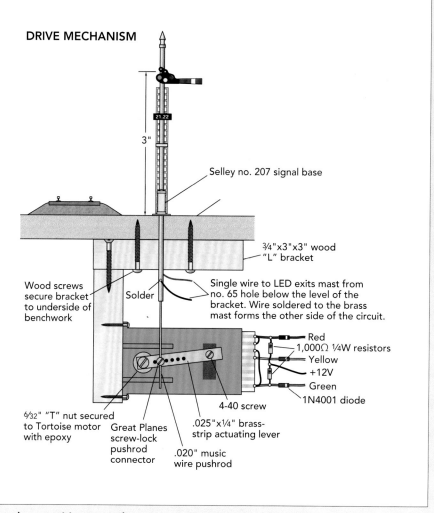

DRIVE MECHANISM

3"

Selley no. 207 signal base

¾"x3"x3" wood "L" bracket

Wood screws secure bracket to underside of benchwork

Solder

Single wire to LED exits mast from no. 65 hole below the level of the bracket. Wire soldered to the brass mast forms the other side of the circuit.

Red
1,000Ω ¼W resistors
Yellow
+12V
Green
1N4001 diode

4-40 screw

.025"x¼" brass-strip actuating lever

⁶∕₃₂" "T" nut secured to Tortoise motor with epoxy

Great Planes screw-lock pushrod connector

.020" music wire pushrod

47

Jeff Scherb built this mechanism for driving a three-position semaphore using a Tortoise switch machine.

brass strip. A 4-40 screw through a hole in one end of the lever attaches the lever to the Tortoise actuator. A "T" nut secured to the Tortoise casing and another screw provide the pivot point for the lever. Several ¹∕₁₆" holes drilled through the lever provide a range of adjustment for setting the proper distance of motion. A Great Planes GPMQ3870 screw-lock pushrod connector provides the anchor on the actuating lever for the blade pushrod.

To mount the Tortoise under the layout, make an "L" bracket from ¾" pine. Dimensions for this bracket will depend on whatever obstructions you need to

clear under the layout.

The wiring is quite simple, and requires only two resistors and three diodes. When the green input is grounded, current flows from +12V through R2 to the motor to ground. When the red input is grounded, current flows from +12V through R1 to the motor to ground. When the yellow input is grounded, current flows through R1 or R2 and the SPDT switches depending on the current position of the switch motor, but the motion always will be toward the center. When the switch breaks contact in the center of travel, the motor will stop, giving us the center position.

Diodes D1, D2, and D3 prevent reverse voltages from flowing back through the motor and into the signal logic circuit. This wiring should be compatible with any three-color-signal logic circuit that provides a grounded output. Any circuit that has outputs for red, yellow, and green, where each output goes to ground to light its light, should work just fine.

The color-light circuit Jeff Scherb presented in "Simple circuits for automatic block signals" in the March 2001 *Model Railroader* can be used with semaphores. To use that circuit, resistors R1, R4, and R6 should be 470Ω, ½W, and the supply

voltage should be 12 volts to provide proper drive for the Tortoise.

Also, using that circuit means you can mix and match semaphores with color-light and searchlight signals in the same system. To complete the wiring, a 1KΩ, ¼W resistor should be wired in series with the white LED to limit the current to safe levels for the LED.

Even if you don't have the electronics for a signal system, you can install semaphore signals and wire them to be operated manually. A three-position rotary switch can be used to connect each of the green, yellow, and red terminals of the semaphore circuit to ground.

Appendix B:
List of Manufacturers

All Electronics
14928 Oxnard St.
Van Nuys, CA 91411
www.allelectronics.com

Atlas Model Railroad Co.
378 Florence Ave.
Hillside, NJ 07205
www.atlasrr.com

Aztec Manufacturing Co.
2701 Conestoga Drive, Unit 113
Carson City, NV 89706
www.aztectrains.com

Boulder Creek Engineering, LLC
2525 Arapahoe Ave.
Suite E4-605
Boulder CO 80302
www.bouldercreekengineering.com

Circuitron, Inc.
211 RocBaar Dr.
Romeoville, IL 60446-1163
www.circuitron.com

CVP Products
P.O. Box 835772
Richardson, TX 75083-5772
www.cvpusa.com

DCC Specialties
57 River Rd, Suite 1023
Essex Junction, VT 05452
www.dccspecialties.com

Deltang
On30guy.gerenm.net

Digi-Key Corporation
701 Brooks Ave. S.
Thief River Falls, MN 56701
www.digikey.com

Digitrax
2443 Transmitter Rd.
Panama City, FL 32404-3157
www.digitrax.com

Heathcote Electronics
1 Haydock Close, Cheadle
Staffordshire, ST10 1UE
www.heathcote-electronics.co.uk

Jameco Electronics
1355 Shoreway Rd.
Belmont, CA 94002
www.jameco.com

JLC Enterprises Inc.
P.O. Box 88187
Grand Rapids, MI 49518
www.jlcenterprises.net

JMRI
jmri.sourceforge.net

Kadee Quality Products Co.
673 Avenue C
White City, OR 97503-1078
www.kadee.com

Lenz Agency of North America
57 River Road, Suite 1023
Essex Junction, VT 05452
www.lenzusa.com

Logic Rail Technologies
21175 Tomball Parkway, Suite 287
Houston, TX 77070
www.logicrailtech.com

Loksound
ESU LLC
477 Knopp D.
Muncy, PA 17756
www.esu.eu

Micro-Mark
www.micromark.com

Miniatronics
561-K Acorn Street
Deer Park, NY 11729
www.miniatronics.com

Model Railroad Electronic Circuits
home.cogeco.ca/~rpaisley4/CircuitIndex.html

Model Rectifier Corporation
80 Newfield Ave.
Edison, NJ 08837
www.modelrectifier.com

Mouser Electronics
11433 Woodside Ave.
Santee, CA 92071 USA
www.mouser.com

NCE Corporation
82 East Main St.
Webster, NY 14580
www.ncedcc.com

National Model Railroad Association
P.O. Box 1328
Soddy Daisy, TN 37384-1328
www.nmra.org

QSI
www.qsisolutions.com

Radio Shack
www.radioshack.com

Richmond Controls
P.O. Box 1467
Richmond, TX 77406-1467
www.richmondcontrols.com

RR-CirKits, Inc.
7918 Royal Ct.
Waxhaw, NC 28173
www.rr-cirkits.com

SoundTraxx
210 Rock Point Dr.
Durango, CO 81301
www.soundtraxx.com

Stanton S-cab
www.s-cab.com

Streamlined Backshop
7229 Euliss Ct.
Avon, IN 46123
www.sbs4dcc.com

Tam Valley Depot
4541 Hidalgo Ave.
San Diego, CA 92117
www.tamvalleydepot.com

Team Digital, LLC
3111 Timber Valley Dr.
Kokomo, IN 46902
www.teamdigital1.com

Tony's Trains
Pinewood Plaza
57 River Rd, Suite 1023
Essex Jct, VT 05452
www.tonystrains.com

Train Control Systems
P.O. Box 341
Blooming Glen, PA 18911
www.tcsdcc.com

Wm. K. Walthers, Inc.
5601 W. Florist Ave.
Milwaukee, WI 53218-1622
www.walthers.com

Wiring for DCC
www.wiringfordcc.com

About the author

Dr. Larry Puckett is a retired scientist living in Asheville, N.C., with his wife, Diane. Professionally, Larry worked as a research ecologist with the U.S. Geological Survey for 33 years, studying water quality. During that time he also served for six years as an associate editor of the *Journal of Environmental Quality*.

Larry served as a contributing editor for *Model Railroading* magazine from 1991 until 2006 and his DCC Updates column ran there for 11 years. He has more than 170 articles to his credit in that magazine as well as in *Model Railroader, Model Railroading,* and *Railroad Model Craftsman*. He has written extensively on the subject of Digital Command Control and his book *Practical Guide to Digital Command Control* was published by Carstens Publications in 2008 and is now available from White River Publications. Since February 2015, Larry has been the DCC Corner columnist for *Model Railroader*.

Like many model railroaders his age, Larry's introduction to model trains came with an O gauge set that he received for Christmas in 1958; however, his introduction to trains goes back even further. Larry's grandfather worked for the Norfolk & Western Railway, and as a toddler he and his mother often rode the N&W Bluefield-to-Norton passenger train into town on shopping trips. It shouldn't come as a surprise that his main modeling interests include railroads of the southeastern United States, particularly the Southern and N&W, which are the focus of his current Piedmont Southern layout. He says he became a serious modeler in 1980 after purchasing a copy of *Model Railroader* at a local hobby shop.

"I've always been a history buff and I enjoy researching how prototype railroads operated and then applying that to my model railroading," Larry said. "I also enjoy the technical side of the hobby, especially the electronics, which has always been useful when working with Digital Command Control. The introduction of DCC has not only radically changed how we wire our model railroads, it has changed how we operate them as well. So for me the electronics goes hand in hand with prototype operations."

When not in his train room or pecking out a DCC Corner column on his computer, Larry enjoys landscape photography and fly fishing for native and wild trout in the many mountain streams of western North Carolina.

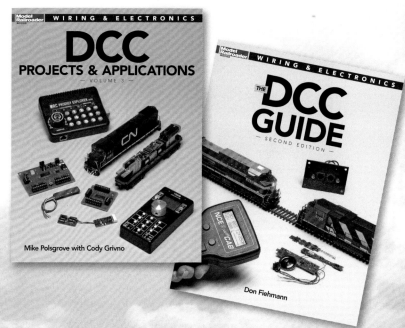